Spin-Off **MAGAZINE PRESENTS**

HANDSPUN TREASURES
from RARE WOOLS

Collected Works from the Save the Sheep Project

Edited by Deborah Robson

INTERWEAVE PRESS

...ntage of the profits from this book is being ... the American Livestock Breeds Conservancy.

The American Livestock   Breeds Conservancy

Photography, except where otherwise credited, by Joe Coca
Production and cover design by Dean Howes

Interweave Press
201 East Fourth Street
Loveland, Colorado 80537
USA

Printed in the United States by Kendall Printing

Library of Congress Cataloging-in-Publication Data

Spin-off magazine presents handspun treasures from rare wools : collected works from the Save the sheep project / edited by Deborah Robson.
     p. cm.
    Includes index.
    ISBN 1-883010-84-5
     1. Hand spinning—Exhibitions. 2. Sheep breeds—Exhibitions. 3. Rare breeds—Exhibitions. I.Title: Handspun treasures from rare wools. II. Robson, Deborah. III. Spin-off (Loveland, Colo.)

TT847 .S675 2000
746.1'2—dc21   00-033602

First printing:IWP:5M:0500:KP

For more information on conservation of livestock breeds, including sheep, contact:

American Livestock Breeds Conservancy
P.O. Box 477
Pittsboro, North Carolina 27312
(919) 542-5704 voice
(919) 545-0022 fax
www.albc-usa.org
albc@albc-usa.org

ALBC is a nonprofit organization and contributions are tax-deductible.

On front cover

Clockwise from top left:

Four-month-old, four-horned Jacob ewe lamb, courtesy of Mary Spahr, Spahr Farm, Jamestown, Ohio.

"Turtledove in Red," by Ellen Sullivan, made of Navajo Churro wool.

Leicester Longwool ewe and ram, Abigail on left and Little Man on right, courtesy of Katie McLaughlin, Tazewell, Virginia.

Scarf, by Brenda Bryon, of Wensleydale wool.

Shetland ram, courtesy of Sue Edwards, Inverurie, Aberdeenshire, Scotland.

Flock sweater, by Teresa Gardner, of Shetland wool.

On back cover

Teeswater, courtesy of David W. Ward, The Teeswater Sheep Breeder's Association, North Yorkshire, United Kingdom.

Scarf and cap by Heather Maxey, of Manx Loghtan wool.

CONTENTS

This book is dedicated to

the shepherds

and to all the spinners
who make magic with their hands

Cotswold

Mittens

Noreen Muellerweiss
Michigan

&

Emerald City Dog Lead

Catherine Reimers

& Nancy Bertino
New York

Teeswater

Rug

Nanette Mosher
Illinois

Shetland

Fair Isle Vest

Liz Johnson
Utah

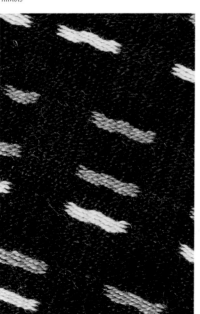

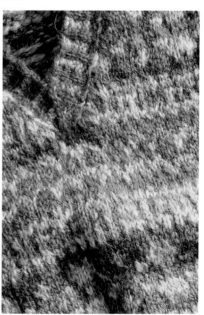

PREFACE

This journey began for me about twenty-five years ago, when I picked up a spindle and a handful of raw Dorset wool and began trying to make yarn. The experiment worked, and I'm still on that path. (Note to beginners: practice while standing next to a bed and your dropped spindle will be much easier to retrieve repeatedly.)

The odyssey shifted to its second phase fourteen years ago, when I learned that Navajo Churro sheep—they seemed exotic at the time because I hadn't touched the wool or met this kind of sheep—were approaching extinction. The third phase? Reading the lists of endangered breeds prepared by The American Livestock Breeds Conservancy and the Rare Breeds Survival Trust, I realized that they resembled a "who's who" of handspinners' materials, spiced with a few unfamiliar names connected to wools that I've since had the delight of experiencing. I hope my daughter and other younger spinners also have that chance.

The fourth phase clicked into place with the Save the Sheep project, sponsored by *Spin-Off* magazine. From this we have developed a traveling fine-craft exhibit (perhaps the first featuring exclusively handspun work); a slide show presenting many handspun pieces made with rare-breed wools; five collections of fabric swatches which convey information about these fibers, their heritage, and their potential; and this book, which presents an overview of all those endeavors.

The fifth phase? Back to my spindle, with a smorgasbord of fibers at hand. The trip's just begun.

Deborah Robson

Jacob
Throw
Linda Geiger
spinner
Joan Berner
weaver
New York

RARE BREEDS & SPINNERS

by Deborah Robson

Galway
Ewe, Co. Galway.
Photo courtesy of Anne-Marie Moroney.

Handspinners are in a unique position to understand the value of many of the sheep breeds currently designated as rare, critical, or endangered. Our expertise lies in assessment of one aspect of a sheep—its wool. Other groups of people who are weighing the strengths of breeds which have become marginal and in need of conservation have different priorities, including meat quality and yield, prolificacy, and nutritional requirements. To them, wool is a byproduct, often called the "second crop" (after meat).[1] To us, it is paramount.

If we have an interest in maintaining the diversity of the wools which are available—colors, textures, lengths, fineness or coarseness, crimp patterns— we need to become knowledgeable about the status of all breeds of sheep, and to vote with our voices (and, as we buy fiber, our checkbooks) in favor of those qualities of fiber we'd like to see preserved.

Questions arose as we proceeded with the Save the Sheep project, the purpose of which is to promote understanding about rare sheep breeds within and beyond the spinning community. Many of the issues raised by this effort affect wild animals and other domesticated species as well as sheep, but sheep will be our primary reference point.

In our practice of this craft, it doesn't make sense for spinners to use only fibers grown by rare-breed sheep. When we look deeply enough at the issues involved, we find that all of traditional agriculture (like wilderness) is endangered by the spread of lawns, pavement, and pollution. Whether the label says endangered or not, we need to pay attention. Now. In the case of spinning, that paying of attention can result in the enormous pleasure of discovery and learning. It can also support the breeders who have so far kept these resources available for us.

We believe that a diversity of fiber types is essential to conserving the full range of skills and cultural values embodied by our craft. And the sheep breeds we have focused on in this project clearly need our most immediate support and appreciation.

[1]A few breeds offer a third product: milk.

Note: A version of this article originally appeared in *Spin-Off* 23, no. 1 (Spring 1999), pages 90–93.

What is a breed?

You'd think this would be an easy question to answer. It isn't. There is no black-and-white definition of *breed*. It's a working principle, an idea in motion.

The word is easy enough to use, and from usage we come upon what will have to pass for a definition. One of the simplest nuggets comes from *A Rare Breeds Album of American Livestock,* which says "breeds breed true." This sounds like, "If it looks like a duck, walks like a duck, and quacks like a duck, then it is a duck." Well, yes. The offspring within a breed resemble the parents in ways which are visible (wool quality, conformation, eye color) and also in ways that are not apparent to the naked eye (resistance to parasites, tendency to give birth without assistance, ability to survive adverse conditions).

Midway between random sheepdom and an acknowledged breed is the *type.* Types arise from crossbreeding (of which more will be said later) and manifest characteristics within a range which is broader than that of a breed. You can guess reasonably well what the offspring of a mating will look like and what other qualities it will embody, yet the genetic range has not been defined as clearly as it is in the breed.

Some identifiable groups of local sheep (for example, those which support traditional textile crafts in Chiapas, Mexico) can be called types, rather than breeds. In the future, if desired characteristics have been stabilized and breeding is controlled so that those characteristics predictably occur in offspring, the descendants of these groups of sheep might end up being called members of a breed.

How does a breed get to be a breed? First, humans limit the selection of animals who will be allowed to mate for long enough that the results of breeding can be predicted. Once the results have been stabilized, humans maintain the group's identity by continuing to control breeding within the group and the established parameters.

Some breeds are more uniform than others. Just as breed status is conferred by human arbiters, the allowable range of variation is determined by human standards. The boundaries (who's "in" and who's "out") can be set for utilitarian, aesthetic, political, or other reasons, and those boundaries can shift over time. As an example, Jacob sheep in the United Kingdom have changed to meet broader market needs (for one thing, they're larger and produce more meat per animal than they used to) and are not on a conservation list. Jacob sheep in North America have been preserved in a state closer to the breed's earlier form, and are classified as rare.

Hebridean
Ewe on the island of North Uist in the Hebrides.
Photo courtesy of Eric Medway, Hebridean Sheep Society.

Why some breeds are rare

Sheep were originally domesticated about 15,000 years ago, yet the question of rare breeds and the need for conservation efforts have only arisen in the very recent past—say the last twenty years, in terms of organized effort to preserve genetic potential, and perhaps the last hundred, in terms of dawning awareness that individual breeds were at risk. As extinction hovers equally around species (of wild creatures) and breeds (of domesticated ones), humans are attempting to maintain biological diversity in the face of daunting odds and diminishing environments.

Sheep become rare through a conjunction of two forces.

First there is economic pressure, which promotes a handful of breeds at the expense of the rest. Particular breeds are perceived to have characteristics useful in the current economic system, and most ambitious raisers of livestock sensibly invest their resources in these animals. Other breeds decrease in numbers. Perceived value depends upon a complex interaction of genetics, husbandry practices, and marketing goals, and is subject to change with shifts in availability of resources (ready access to antibiotics or to grain, as opposed to pasture) or in what the public considers desirable (say, for the dairy industry, high or low butterfat content).

In the matter of wool, the "public" has considered medium-grade wool the "best" fiber since industrial spinning equipment started to produce more textiles than craftworkers did. Many sheep breeds are described today in terms of their meat production, with the adjunct comment that the wool is "acceptable" or "adequate."

Second comes the awareness that a breed is at risk of vanishing entirely. At this point, a watchdog group steps in and begins damage control. Groups which monitor the status of breeds and work for their conservation are still in the formative stages, and they work against the tide of dominant economic forces. Even those with the most extended histories and greatest successes to date—like The American Livestock Breeds Conservancy (ALBC) in North America and the Rare Breeds Survival Trust (RBST) in the United Kingdom—have been active for less than thirty years.

It's shocking to realize how quickly a breed can disappear. Assume that a sheep's lifespan may be about ten years. Within less than ten years of a decision (conscious or otherwise) to cease producing purebreds of a given breed, the breed as a whole will be gone. To re-establish a breed, on the other hand, may or may not be feasible. It is at best a random process with uncertain and unverifiable results, and requires many generations of dedicated and perceptive husbandry.

Leicester Longwool
Photo courtesy of Colonial Williamsburg Foundation.

Who decides what's rare, and how?

A decision about the vulnerability of a set of breeds requires a decision-making body, a list of the breeds to be considered, and records of the sheep that currently exist. It's easier to find decision-making bodies than comprehensive lists of breeds or accurate census data.

Groups like ALBC and RBST and the United Nations' Domestic Animal Diversity project (sponsored by the Food and Agriculture Organization) are scrambling to compile lists, tally animals, and determine which situations need crisis management and which require simple monitoring. This is a moving-target project, and the speed at which the target moves would discourage the faint-hearted. In addition, the accuracy of the organizations' data varies—especially for the U.N. project, since many of the contributing countries and regions have more immediate problems to solve than the counting of sheep.

The criteria for classification also vary from group to group, although the principles guiding the development of criteria collect around a predictable group of factors. These include the number of females which are being bred true, the number of male lines being used for breeding (a crucial element in conserving a viable population), and the number and location of flocks.

Some groups focus on population figures within their geographic areas, while others place equal or greater emphasis on global populations. When considering global resources, it's important to acknowledge the interaction between animal and environment, as well as the speed and power with which local selection processes can shift a population's identity. Groups of sheep called by the same name in different locations may have distinct identities. Karakuls are widespread throughout the world, but are identified and protected as a rare

Villsau (Old Norwegian)
Baby Socks
Trygve Fjarli & Ruth Volden
Norway

Villsau (Old Norwegian)
Left, adults. Above, lamb. Photos courtesy of Trygve Fjarli.

breed in North America. Populations of Karakuls elsewhere may be identified as breed or as type when more data are collected.

The United Nations group is attempting to collect information on all the domestic livestock in the world—a daunting task, and like other jobs which require gathering massive quantities of details from diverse sources, it's one that the Internet is facilitating, perhaps even making possible. Faced with hundreds of breeds in many species, the U.N.'s classification criteria are more stringent than those of other organizations. In large part, the U.N.'s Domestic Animal Diversity (DAD) conservation goals depend on the efforts of regional groups. The DAD database seems to breathe an electronic sigh of relief (and pull that breed off its endangered list) when a breed's vulnerability is acknowledged by people in a position to take action on its behalf. To put this succinctly: if a breed is listed as endangered by the U.N., it's in dire shape. Breeds on the DAD list are counted "not at risk" if there's someone on the scene trying to save it, however meager their hope of succeeding.

Groups like ALBC and RBST monitor their areas closely, re-crunch new data on a regular basis, and issue bulletins on the survival status of the breeds they're watching. Their actions on behalf of sheep are limited, however, because of the numbers of species they monitor. Sheep are one concern among many, and the groups' time needs to be distributed where it's most needed, moment by moment.

Crossbreeds

Crossbreeding—producing animals by mating individuals from different breeds—serves many useful purposes, both in the individual offspring and for the wider world of sheep. At the individual level, crosses can combine qualities of different breeds to produce specific results and can offer the benefits of hybrid vigor, where growth of wool or meat exceeds that which would be expected from pure-breeding. (It's worth noting that hybrid vigor is greatest when the parents are not from similar genetic backgrounds.) In the wider sense, of course, careful crossbreeding can provide the foundation work for the development of new breeds.

As a means of conserving the genetic potential in a given breed, however, crossbreeding is of extremely limited value. A few geneticists argue in favor of melding all the minor breeds into a generalized "gene pool," on the theory that at some point in the future we'll have the ability to extract from this pool the genes—or, more often, complex combinations of genes—that are needed to produce animals of specific configurations and strengths. Despite recent major advances in genetic research, the skills required to do this still rest firmly in the realm of science fiction.

In the interim, although a crossbred lamb carries genetic information from both its parents, the result is a lot like storing sugar and salt in the

Cotswold
Bad Hair Day
Anne Williams
Connecticut

same canister. You can't bake a reliable cake or loaf of bread without separating the two substances. It is possible to sort salt from sugar with current knowledge and equipment, although the job would be tedious at best. For genetic information, we don't know what to sort or how to recombine the components, and we don't have the tools that would let us begin the job, much less finish it.

Why does this matter to spinners?

We—humans, that is—can't save everything. There's some hope that we can save a significant amount of the currently available genetic potential, assuming that we can reduce the pressure on habitats (agricultural as well as wild) at the same time that we determine priorities and means of conservation.

Are all breeds equally valuable? Probably not, and if you look at the rare breeds only from the standpoint of the wool they currently produce, a few would not seem worth saving. Hair sheep produce fiber that we'd spin only for novelty, or as part of an artistic piece that makes a political statement, or to increase our appreciation for other fibers. Some wool-growing breeds produce fleeces we'd consider strictly mediocre, if that.

But other qualities of those particular sheep may be important for other reasons in the future, and they may carry genes which would support the development of a new breed which could survive—perhaps even thrive— under conditions which would destroy all others, or which might contribute a type of fiber we'd hate to do without

Humans don't know everything (although sometimes we think we know enough to pretend we do), and we can't make fully informed decisions on topics as broad as genetic conservation. But we can help prevent losses that we're likely to regret deeply. Here are a few examples of what spinners stand to lose if the rare breeds of sheep are abandoned to extinction, which is their certain fate if people who care about them don't intervene, to whatever degree they are able.

Consider color. With a few exceptions, the genes for colored wool are carried by sheep of breeds currently classed as rare. Color in fleece is determined not by one set of genes but by a combination, in which white is strongly dominant and black most often is readily overruled. The genetic configuration required to produce brown involves such a combination of other genes stepping out of the way that it's a wonder we have any brown wool at all, much less its shades. Rare breeds produce a disproportionate number of colored fleeces because their genetic pools are replete with the necessary—and notably recessive—genes.

Traditionally, the wide variety of wools has supported a broad array of craft techniques and artistic forms. Some wools felt well, while others do not. The finest wools can be used for underwear, the coarsest for rugs and

Cotswold
Left, ewe named April. Right, ram named King Lear. Both fairly recently shorn. Photo courtesy of Anne Williams.

California Variegated Mutant
Kerry Blue Shawl
Diane Bentley-Baker
Texas

California Variegated Mutant
Flora's Socks
Robin Lynde
California

California Variegated Mutant
Mogollon Shawl
Jacquie Kelly
Arizona

camel trappings and cords. All of the extremes—the wools which are *superior* for one use or another, not just adequate or acceptable—are vulnerable as we contemplate the loss of the rare sheep breeds.

Since domesticated animals provide so many different benefits to human culture, groups of people with varying biases will have divergent ideas about what's most valuable and what's at greatest risk. Unless handspinners speak to the qualities of the fiber, and support a small but steady market for it, only the machines' needs will be considered in the types of wool that are produced in the future. At the very least, we owe it to ourselves—now, while we can—to teach our fingers the ways of working with wools outside our comfort zone and expertise, so we can help make informed decisions about what we treasure enough that we want to be sure it's still around when we discover we needed it after all.

Deborah Robson edited Spin-Off: The Magazine for Handspinners *for more than a dozen years. She has been a spinner since 1974, and loves discovering how textiles work in themselves and in relation to people, animals, and environments.*

Here's a successful

experiment in making the most of different wools, using their subtleties to enhance the construction and wearing characteristics of a garment. Catherine Reimers began without a plan, testing the fibers, paying attention to their special qualities as she spun, and thinking about the role each wool could play in this sweater for a young person.

The California Variegated Mutant (CVM) and Shetland fulled well, so she put them in the body where they provide a stable base for the embroidery. Her full sleeves are soft Tunis. The Jacob became a fine embroidery yarn, which she dyed with indigo.

Her embroidery is loosely inspired by borage blossoms that still flourished in her garden in November and that she says are "a symbol of my wish that these old breeds, too, may thrive."

California Variegated Mutant, Jacob, Shetland, & Tunis
Borage Blossom Sweater
Catherine Reimers
New York

Jean Newsted's Santa

shows in a small space how different wools suit different purposes. His boots and belt are soft, shiny Teeswater. The fur trim on his clothes is super-soft, matte-surfaced North Ronaldsay. His hands and face are soft Shetland. His hair and beard are bouncy, wavy Cotswold (the shine is a bonus). Body and clothes are lustrous yet strong Wensleydale ("just right for many trips down chimneys"), and his pack is a naturally tan Manx Loghtan.

Jean obtained her colors through both acid and natural dyes, including madder and logwood. She prepared all the wools on five-pitch wool combs, and adapted her pattern from an original in Jean Greenhowe's *Christmas Special* (Aberdeen, Scotland: Jean Greenhowe Designs, 1991).

Cotswold, Manx Loghtan, North Ronaldsay, Shetland, Teeswater, & Wensleydale
A Spinner's Santa
Jean Newsted
Alberta, Canada

Rare Sheep Breeds

by D. P. Sponenberg, D.V.M., Ph.D., and D. E. Bixby, D.V.M.

How they got that way, and why it matters

Each of the beautiful and significant works in the Save the Sheep project springs from a talented craftsperson encountering wool produced by specific breeds of sheep. These breeds and their fibers have inspired the creative work you see in these pages. Its importance goes way beyond the obvious beauty and utility of the objects themselves.

The American Livestock Breeds Conservancy (ALBC) is delighted with the results of this competition, and with the increased awareness it provides for breed conservation in the United States. Familiarity with the background of breeds and their conservation can only increase the appreciation and significance of this exhibition, and presenting that background is one of the reasons for ALBC's existence.

The Save the Sheep competition and exhibition exquisitely highlight the incredible variety and beauty of wools from rare sheep breeds, and attest to the significance of these breeds. Save the Sheep also sparks some very good questions: What is a breed anyway? Why are some breeds rare? Why does any of this matter?

The concept of breed can be a tricky one. Breeds are a category limited to domesticated animals. Breeds in domesticated animals are similar, but not identical, to subspecies in wild animals. Breeds are an interesting and important offshoot of the entire domestication process. They reflect the varied and vital partnerships between people and animals.

Breeds are reasonably uniform and predictable genetic packages, which means that members of a breed resemble one another enough to be logically grouped in the same population. When members of the same breed are mated, their offspring are of the same type as the parents. This is a dry statement of a powerful genetic fact: breeds are predictable genetic resources. Locked within these few concepts are glimpses of the entire past history of agriculture and of human interaction with domesticated animals. Our relationship with sheep is long and intricate, and has been incredibly beneficial to both sheep and people.

Breeds developed genetic consistency as a result of their journey through history, during which they were exposed to combinations of isolation and selection. The selection pressures included those imposed by nature, as well as by human preferences. Stefan Adalsteinsson, an Icelander who has been instrumental in saving and documenting many Scandinavian breeds, refers to today's breeds as having a genetic heritage of survival. In this statement, he thoughtfully conveys that when we look at a breed today we are looking at the end product of the entire history of that breed—where it lived, how it survived the hardships it experienced, how it was valued, what it produced, and how it participated in this wonderful relationship with humans. Breeds are living representatives of complicated and intertwined factors that acted on them in the past. Locked within a breed's genes are its responses to these events and pressures. Each breed is a living record of its unique past. The wonderful diversity of breeds represents the multitude of different situations in which sheep found themselves, adapted, and survived.

Specific sheep breeds are shaped both by their environment and by what their owners favor. The physical environment and the human caretakers both make demands on the sheep, and each breed has answered these demands in slightly different ways. Over millennia, this has caused the original animal known as a sheep to diversify into a multitude of breeds. Each breed reflects the sum of the demands placed on it by a specific environment and production system. Consequently, each breed has its own look and style, and its own characteristic wool. Each is a unique record of what happened when sheep, people, and the physical environment overlapped.

The relationship between people and sheep is ancient. Until very recently, sheep breeding was a local phenomenon in which talented and astute humans assessed the sheep in their vicinity for desirable characteristics. This system tailored available animals to the environment as well as to production goals for fiber type. Animals first had to survive. Then those which provided especially valued products were selectively maintained and reproduced. In their most extreme manifestations, these local systems produce the highly adapted genetic packages that we know today as breeds. In portions of Europe, we still find excellent examples of diverse, highly specialized, local types, each of which represents millennia of interaction between humans, sheep, and an environment.

A quick overview of sheep at the end of the 1800s would have revealed an incredible number of locally distributed breeds, each a unique representation of local cultural and environmental conditions. They included breeds for desert use, for marshy lowlands, or for humid tropical areas; breeds with lustrous wool, fine wool, or only hair with no wool at all; breeds with short bare tails, and others with long, fatty tails weighing up to forty pounds (18 kg)! The diversity in sheep is amazing, and each unique breed package provided its human caretakers with important responses to survival.

Enter the twentieth century, as transportation and communication accelerate monumentally, crashing in on local communities and hurling them into a more global and widely interconnected society. Extremes become lost, and the prevailing trend sort of averages the diverse components going into

Santa Cruz Island
Opposite page: Elsa, a two-week-old lamb, just before she was rescued by Signe Swenson and her husband. Above, bottom to top: Elsa and a ram, rescued at the same time, age two months. Elsa and Signe. Photos courtesy of Nancy Van Tassel.

the mix. Communities, no longer bound by local constraints, become free to sample and choose among many options, including sheep breeds available worldwide.

Instead of appreciating the wealth of alternatives, the agricultural mainstream has chosen to focus on a few breeds, which now dominate animal production systems. These few breeds perform well in benign or controlled environments, conditioned by high levels of inputs—high-quality feed, veterinary care, and human intervention. As we reach the start of the twenty-first century, these few breeds' levels of productivity in optimal environments have become the benchmarks against which all other breeds, regardless of environment, have been measured.

As agriculture has changed from highly adapted and locally based production to a system where environments are generalized and support materials like food and medications are brought from the outside, so has the breed array changed. Adaptation and survival have become dramatically less appreciated than overall production. For United States sheep, production of meat has been emphasized. In many breeds, wool quality receives very little support and attention. The development of synthetic fibers has accelerated the discounting of the importance of wool. Traditional and local textiles and their production techniques have also gone by the wayside, taking with them the appreciation for distinctive fibers and the breeds that produce those wools.[1]

Unique local management techniques have been lost, and the result has been an averaging of both environments and production systems. Local,

far left
Navajo Churro
Vest, detail
D. Phillip Sponenberg
Virginia

left
Navajo Churro
Shawl
Kathrin Olson-Rutz
Montana

successful strategies are discarded in favor of an acceptably productive composite. This process has brought many breeds to very rare status. That rarity endangers the unique adaptations that these breeds hold.

Each rare sheep breed is rare for a reason, and each has a slightly different story which accounts for its falling fortunes. Some reasons spring from modern production goals—several rare breeds consist of animals too small in body size to meet present market demands, or they grow fiber which goes through mainstream commercial wool-processing channels poorly, if at all. Other breeds hit management constraints, and still others simply fall out of vogue for reasons more related to show-ring or market fads than to any inherent deficiency in production capability.

Sheep breeds that are tailored for extreme environments with minimal inputs—which thrive under the care of peripheral, local cultures—are especially likely to become rare. Navajo Churro sheep are a good example of a breed shaped by close interaction with humans in a challenging environment. As mainstream America hurried down its path to prosperity and success, many cultures and situations in isolated regions were simply left out, to varying degrees. This resulted in little appreciation for these sheep, for their role in their original location, and for the products they offered.

Not only are the causes of rarity unique to each breed, but the reversal of the fortunes of these rare gems is also unique to each breed. For most breeds, a few consistent phenomena have prevailed and have been able to turn around their declines. For many of the rare breeds, an array of people has rallied support and promotion. Each breed has a unique cast of characters that has assured breed survival, and without whom the breed would be doomed. The American Livestock Breeds Conservancy works with these individuals and organized groups of breeders, and firmly holds that since breeders gave us breeds, breeders are their best hope for survival. People and sheep remain inextricably intertwined throughout breed development, through the decline to rarity, and also through recovery and conservation.

One factor that unifies the conservation of sheep, when compared to other species, is the wide range of wool types that rare-breed sheep produce. These fibers are, in many cases, anathema to the mainstream wool industry. However, they are a godsend to fiber artists. Each wool has a best use, and the fiber artist is able to tailor the project to the type of wool. Projects ranging from lace shawls to hardwearing rugs demand different wools, and those different wools are produced (consistently and predictably!) by different breeds. As contemporary interest in fiber crafts has proliferated, so has the demand for wools of a wide range of types and styles.

Navajo Churro
Ewe (Josephine) and lambs. Photo courtesy of John Hopkins, The Jade Cat Studios, Hobbs, New Mexico.

---

[1]*Editor's note:* On this point, see in particular Priscilla Gibson-Roberts' work, on page 40.

Increased demand for different wools can greatly help conserve rare breeds, but this path to conservation is not without challenges. Many types of wool can be produced by crossbred, as well as purebred, sheep. Once a fleece has been shorn, it can be difficult to assess whether the sheep which grew the wool was purebred and useful for conservation, or crossbred and only useful for its immediate product. Fiber artists working with wool therefore need to be informed about the source of their material and about its importance to this effort, so that wools provided by purebred sheep find a brisk market and reward breeders for conserving these genetic treasures. To do otherwise is to eventually lose these unique resources. The Save the Sheep project has greatly aided the recognition and marketing of pure rare-breed wools, and has established a potential longstanding trend for fiber artists.

Each rare breed has its niche, its unique products, its own story of development, and then its own array of factors leading to declining fortunes. Each breed also has behind it a few key proponents who value it and foster its use by others. The dedicated work of these few visionaries has enabled these breeds to survive so far. Their efforts have brought these genetic packages to the present day for us to enjoy and use. Their work needs to be recognized as vital for all of us, and needs to be supported and expanded so that these breeds do not disappear.

The American Livestock Breeds Conservancy recognizes the incredible role that all present and past breed caretakers have had. ALBC realizes that while part of the breed conservation issue rests on rather cold and impersonal biological facts, much of it embodies a rich tapestry of human and animal endeavors, interwoven into a complex fabric which cannot be unraveled to reveal strictly human or strictly animal components. This overlap and interconnection provide much of the mystique of breeds, and also compel us to save them, as a vital part of human experience and potential.

D. P. Sponenberg and Don Bixby have both been involved with The American Livestock Breeds Conservancy since the organization's early years. ALBC was founded in 1977. Don has been its executive director since 1988 and works energetically and constantly for the conservation of rare livestock breeds. Phil, a professor of pathology and genetics at the Virginia-Maryland Regional College of Veterinary Medicine, has a special interest in locally adapted breeds of livestock. The interest extends to his own farm, which is home to Leicester Longwool sheep and Tennessee Fainting goats (they grow a wonderful, fine, spinnable undercoat). He shears, spins, and knits, and enjoys using a variety of wools in his creations.

Reference List of Rare Sheep Breeds

These are the sheep listed as rare, endangered, and minority breeds by The American Livestock Breeds Conservancy (ALBC, North America) and the Rare Breeds Survival Trust (RBST, United Kingdom) at the time of the Save the Sheep project. Each geographic area has its own list, and a few rare breeds from other parts of the world—New Zealand, Germany, and Norway in particular—also are represented in this book.

The breeds listed with asterisks are not shown or described in the Save the Sheep traveling exhibit or this book. A few are represented in the swatches which spinners sent to be used for educational purposes. All warrant further exploration by handspinners—even the hair sheep! For summary information on all the breeds, see "Rare Wools from Rare Sheep, Part 1: A focused tour of breeds and fiber," *Spin-Off* 22, no. 4 (Winter 1998), pages 54–60. For more detailed information, contact The American Livestock Breeds Conservancy or the Rare Breeds Survival Trust at the addresses in the box on the opposite page.

* **Balwen**, Balwen Welsh Mountain (United Kingdom)—RBST, vulnerable
* **Barbados Blackbelly**, a hair sheep (North America)—ALBC, watch
* **Boreray** (United Kingdom)—RBST, feral
California Variegated Mutant (CVM)/Romeldale (North America)—ALBC, critical
* **Castlemilk Moorit** (United Kingdom)—RBST, critical
Cotswold (North America, United Kingdom)—ALBC, rare; RBST, vulnerable
* **Dorset Down** (United Kingdom)—RBST, at risk
Dorset Horn (North America)—ALBC, watch
* **Galway** (United Kingdom)—RBST, endangered
* **Greyface Dartmoor** (United Kingdom)—RBST, at risk
Gulf Coast Native (North America)—ALBC, critical
* **Hebridean** (United Kingdom)—RBST, minority
* **Hill Radnor** (United Kingdom)—RBST, vulnerable
Hog Island (North America)—ALBC, critical
Jacob, American (North America)—ALBC, rare

Karakul, American (North America)—ALBC, rare
* **Katahdin**, a hair sheep (North America)—ALBC, watch
* **Kerry Hill** (United Kingdom)—RBST, minority
Leicester Longwool (North America, United Kingdom)—ALBC, rare; RBST, endangered
Lincoln (United Kingdom)—RBST, at risk
* **Llanwenog** (United Kingdom)—RBST, at risk
Manx Loghtan (United Kingdom)—RBST, at risk
Navajo Churro (North America)—ALBC, rare
* **Norfolk Horn** (United Kingdom)—RBST, endangered
North Ronaldsay (United Kingdom)—RBST, vulnerable
* **Oxford** (North America) and **Oxford Down** (United Kingdom)—ALBC, watch; RBST, minority
* **Portland** (United Kingdom)—RBST, vulnerable
Romeldale, see California Variegated Mutant—ALBC, critical
Ryeland (United Kingdom)—RBST, minority breed
* **Saint Croix**, a hair sheep (North America)—ALBC, rare

Santa Cruz Island (North America)—ALBC, critical
Shetland (North America, United Kingdom)—ALBC, watch; RBST, minority
* **Shropshire** (United Kingdom)—RBST, at risk
Soay (United Kingdom)—RBST, vulnerable
Southdown (United Kingdom)—RBST, at risk
* **South Wales Mountain** (United Kingdom)—RBST, minority
Teeswater (United Kingdom)—RBST, vulnerable
Tunis (North America)—ALBC, rare
Wensleydale (United Kingdom)—RBST, at risk
* **White Park** (United Kingdom)—RBST, endangered
* **White Face Dartmoor** (United Kingdom)—RBST, minority
* **Whitefaced Woodland** (United Kingdom)—RBST, endangered
* **Wiltshire Horn** (North America, United Kingdom)—ALBC, rare; RBST, minority

A GLIMPSE INTO THE HISTORY OF HANDSPINNING

by Susan Strawn Bailey

Shetland
Half-circle Shawl
Beth Caddell
Indiana

Last year in Colombia I acquired a loosely spun rope of sunburned brown and black wool locks from a *campesina* who carried fleece and hand-spun yarn on her back. As she walked from farm to village, she spun yarn with a hand-carved, wooden drop spindle. Back home, I'll spin this finely crimped wool into yarn, too, and I'll knit a shawl. Not because I have to spin and knit to have a shawl. Not because I need more work to do. I'll spin for the touch of washing, carding, and spinning wool that has felt the high-altitude sun of the Andes, wool that holds the rich, lanolin smell of Colombian sheep. I enjoy this feeling of connection with the other human hands that, for thousands of years, touched every fiber during every step in the creation of each piece of handspun cloth.

The long view through history

Handspinning skills meant survival for those ancient people who lived off the land and spun whatever fibers were available to cover themselves against the elements. Some regions of the world provided better fiber resources than others. The Egyptians, blessed with a warm climate and the Nile river valleys, first cultivated flax and cotton for their sophisticated spinning and weaving (some Egyptian cloth is 300 yards/274 m long and has 540 warps per inch/2.5 cm) centuries before people in other parts of the world began to establish textile traditions. Scotland, in contrast, had few natural resources—no silkworms, cotton, or long-haired goats—and the Scots clothed themselves in animal skins until invaders introduced flax and sheep. The ability of sheep to adapt to extreme climates encouraged people to move these animals throughout the world from Central Asia, where sheep were first domesticated.

Throughout history, immigrants who sought land and religious freedom brought with them flax seed and sheep, hand cards and combs, hand spindles or spinning wheels, and the skills to use them. Humble but finely crafted homespun kept pioneers warm in the often isolated and harsh new settlements. The first settlers who moved from Iceland to Canada depended on sheep and handspun for warm, knitted clothing they used as protection against the severe climate. The settlers of Newfoundland's fishing villages raised sheep and secured unspun wool locks within the stitches of knitted handspun mittens to make fleece linings that protected hands from icy salt-water. Well into the twentieth century, many people endured America's Great Depression by reverting to the skills of pioneer days, which included handspinning. People distressed by the economy came together during these hard times to talk, sing, read, or listen to the radio while they prepared fiber and spun. In a market that paid little for wool, handspun clothing meant getting by, and knitted handspun supplemented many farm incomes.

Communal societies who sought religious freedom in new lands often relied on handspun clothing and household linens. The Shakers raised flax, sheep, and even silkworms to help establish self-sufficient communities from New England to Kentucky. The peaceful, solitary life of the Hutterite immigrants in Canada required handspun textiles. Handspinning could also mean survival for such conquered peoples as the Aztecs, who spun and wove immense quantities of cotton garments to maintain peace with their rulers. For other cultures, such as the nations of the Baltics and Eastern Europe, traditional crafts quietly supported ethnic and national identities while those regions were subjected to outside rule. When they regained independent nation status, the people of these countries reclaimed their traditional music and handicrafts, including handspinning.

For other nations, handspinning skills and patriotic pride in wearing handspun clothing helped achieve or assert national independence. The American colonists smuggled sheep into North America to found a local wool industry despite England's protests. Later, during the Revolutionary and Civil Wars, wearing handspun signified patriotism. Irish spinners and weavers developed their linen industry when the British denied them wool. Ghandi encouraged the people of India to achieve independence from Great Britain and its textiles by handspinning their own thread. The Chinese guarded their secrets of silk spinning for over three thousand years.

Although handspinning in such massive quantities may have approached burdensome drudgery for some spinners, the finely crafted handspun clothing and linens that survive in textile collections glow with artistic expression and pride of accomplishment. In many nations that didn't allow women to own property, a dowry of handspun household linens, ritual fabrics, or a national costume could have been a woman's only possessions.

Discoveries and elaborations

The earliest spinners twisted fibers, probably grasses and vines, into long, strong strands by rolling them between their fingers or on a surface. They experimented with whatever fibers were available: human hair, animal fur, rushes and grasses of the rivers and deserts, the inner bark or stem fibers of trees, agave, milkweed, nettles. To keep the strands from untwisting, they

Gute
Ram; ancient Swedish breed. Photo courtesy of Ragnar Edberg, of The Gute Sheep Society (Gutefårets hemsida).

wound them onto a stick, which would become the shaft of the ubiquitous *hand spindle.*

These early spinners discovered that a weight, or *whorl,* attached to the stick—perhaps a piece of clay or mud at first—made the spindle turn faster. They also learned to pull the untwisted fibers to join with the already twisted fibers, a process called *drafting.* If a spinner teased fibers a bit before spinning, she could coax them into a softer mass to gather or wrap around her wrist or onto a forked branch called a *distaff,* which she would tuck under her arm or into her belt. She pulled fibers from her distaff to spin on her hand spindle. This portable and convenient system, considered women's work and a virtuous duty in most cultures, served humanity well for thousands of years.

Ancient burial sites, mosaics, and wall paintings dating to before 3000 B.C. indicate that hand spindles developed spontaneously among different cultures worldwide. A mass of reeled silk from eastern China dating to 2850–2650 B.C. documents early silk spinning. Often only the whorls remain after wooden spindles deteriorate, so archaeologists find decorated clay whorls in Neolithic ruins and stone whorls among the bones and arrowheads of prehistoric dwelling sites. Hand spindles throughout history show imaginative variations, adapted for specific fibers and spinning styles. Spindles vary with the shaft's thickness, length, and shape and with the whorl's density, size, shape, and location on the shaft. Ancient Egyptians designed flax spindles with high whorls. Navajos developed

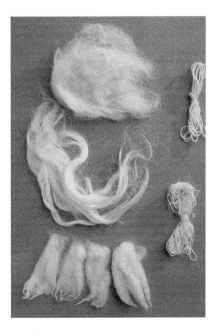

Walachenschaf
Three wool types from
one "primitive" fleece,
with sample yarns

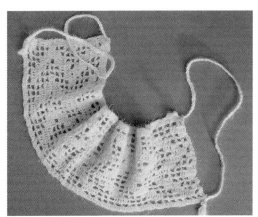

Walachenschaf
Bath Scrubber
Baerbel Epprecht
Germany

large supported spindles which they rotated against the thigh. Hooked sticks have been used in the Sudan, Africa, Asia, and Peru.

Although most prehistoric people did little or no fiber preparation for handspinning, the Egyptians developed complex fiber preparation processes that supported their exquisite flax spinning and weaving. Egyptian tomb paintings dating to 1900 B.C. show assembly lines of slaves, working like human machines in frenetic textile production. Each person performed one of many steps to prepare carded lengths of loosened flax fibers, or *roving*. The roving supplied spinners who wielded two hand spindles at once. In contrast, European women worked as solitary spinners who spun directly from flax or hemp fibers carried on a distaff, instead of from prepared roving.

Handspinning remained essentially unchanged until the invention of the spinning wheel. With its drive wheel, horizontal spindle, and whorl for a pulley, the spinning wheel didn't spin better yarn, but it spun faster. The larger, heavier, more complex spinning wheel didn't displace the simple, convenient hand spindle, but it did require a more settled life. History credits India with the first spinning wheel or *charkha*, some time after A.D. 500. The spinner with this portable Indian wheel sat on the ground and turned a drive wheel which produced a faster rotation than could be obtained with a hand-propelled spindle. In the late Middle Ages, Europeans imported the charkha, enlarged the wheel to spin coarser fibers, and added legs to create what is variously called the *high, wool,* or *walking wheel,* which colonists brought to the New World. The spinner turned the high wheel with one hand and might walk as much as twenty miles in a day of spinning: backward to draft and spin fibers, forward to take up the spun yarn.

Cotswold

The Homeplace 1850 Collection

right

Muffatees (Wrist-warmers) & Cephaline (Cap)

far right

Scarf

The Homeplace 1850 staff members, Jackie Cravens, Cindy Earls, and Amanda Nikkel
Kentucky & Tennessee

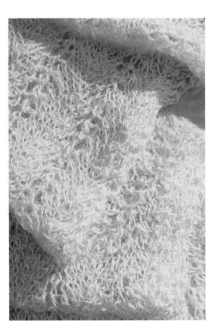

The spinner still had to stop spinning to wind yarn onto the spindle. About 1530, the invention of the first *flyer*, which in one motion inserted twist and wound the yarn onto a bobbin, resolved this dilemma. Once a foot treadle was added to turn the drive wheel, the spinner could use both hands to draft. Inventors and artisans developed variations of the spinning wheel. They also devised useful accessories, including the detachable *distaff* to hold flax or wool, the *swift* to hold and unwind skeins, and the *niddy noddy* (or *wool winder, clock reel, weasel*) to wind yarn into skeins.

Handspinning in the industrial age

The fly-shuttle weaving system, patented in 1733, doubled the speed of weaving and outstripped the capacity of individual spinners to produce thread. This spelled the demise of handspinning as a fundamental activity of daily life. The spinning jenny gave a single spinner the ability to control the production of many ends of yarn at once. It required machine carding, and removed human touch from commercial fiber preparation and spinning for the first time in history.

But not completely. People in developing nations continue their pre-industrial handspinning methods for their own use, for export, and for the tourist trade. Nepali women spin for the Tibetan rug industry. Central and South American farmers spin for artisan weavers and knitters. Navajos spin to enhance the quality of their handwoven rugs and tapestries. Handspinning has changed from a trade to a craft.

The mid-twentieth century also brought a rebirth of interest in hand-spinning to technologically advanced countries. Spinning my Colombian wool connects me with that revival—for the pleasure of touching fiber and wood, for the challenge of spinning a unique yarn, to restore calm in the

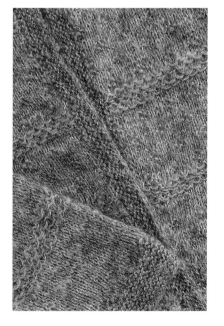

far left
Pommersches Landschaf
Sweater with Brocade Pattern
Patricia Stein
Germany

left
Cotswold
Socks
Noreen Muellerweiss
Michigan

face of a demanding consumer culture that eliminates the necessity for self-sufficiency. Through handspinning, I preserve some ancient resources and knowledge. And I join with other spinners, like the woman in Colombia who harvested this wool I spin, and with millions of spinners who came before me.

Susan Strawn Bailey is an illustrator and writer who contemplates, among other things, the place of everyday textiles in cultural history. If you would like to dig more deeply into the ideas she gathers here, some of her research sources are listed on page 94.

Romeldale
Christening Shawl
Phyllis Karsten
California

Dorset Down
Photo courtesy of Dorset Down Sheep Breeder's Association, Somerset, United Kingdom.

SPINNING FOR EXPRESSION

by Amy C. Clarke

Starting at the beginning

With skilled hands, a spinner takes a handful of fibers and, by twisting them in one direction, transforms the fuzz into a strong thread. Spinning seems pragmatic—the very essence of creating. And yet in its practicality and usefulness, spinning can easily lend itself to metaphor. Spinning is straightforward and basic, and in its simplicity it holds the power of a connection to the past, present, and future. Spinning is a tangible activity, and yet it can allude to a larger, more profound portrait of existence.

After spending thousands of years handspinning, people devised machines that spin yarn—freeing them from the need to create all their yarn by hand. Today's handspinners are not compelled to spin by necessity—now they *choose* to make their own yarn. But what prompts a person to find wool from an endangered breed of sheep, to process it, and to spin it into a yarn that is then woven, knitted, crocheted, or otherwise fashioned into a useful or decorative object? What drives some people to make things from scratch—to start at the very beginning?

 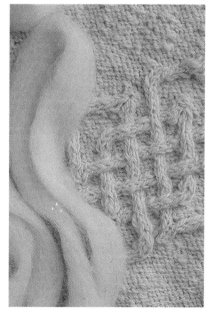

far left & left
Brillenschaf
Viking Sweater
Alexandra Weikert
Germany

For every spinner, you'll find a different reason for spinning. If you ask several spinners why they spin, they may say that it is relaxing, or that they find joy in making things from hand, or maybe that they are able to make yarn exactly as they envision it. And perhaps it goes one step further—maybe they feel that their thoughts and feelings are caught up in the yarn as they spin. Making something from that yarn is powerful.

Spinning and life-force

Some cultures still believe that tying a string around an infant's wrist will prevent the baby's soul from wandering. Others believe that the maze of threads in elaborate embroidery will distract the evil eye and protect the people who wear the clothing. When you raise the sheep, choose their fleece, shear it, clean it, comb it, dye it, and spin it, to knit into a pair of socks for your sweetie—it has to have a different meaning than the socks you pick up off the rack at Wal-Mart.

Portland
Photo courtesy of
Norma Sanders.

Spirals

People have connected the simple act of spinning with powerful meaning for a long time. Paleolithic spindle whorls (the weights that help the spindle spin like a top) were inscribed with spirals, connecting the seemingly magical qualities of spinning with the powerful forces of the universe. In those times, the spiral image was used to express the idea of rebirth. Spirals are dynamic—starting at a single point, the spiral line moves consistently around that point, gradually getting larger and larger. Dualities such as change and repetition, the immense and the minute, and stability and motion, are simultaneously expressed in the spiral. Though static, the spiraling line implies motion and growth. Spiraling patterns surround us in the spider's web, the growth of leaves, and the path of the moon.

The spiral is also a successful tool for describing the patterns of life and death that compose the seasonal changes of the earth. In spring, the dormant ground breaks open as new buds stretch toward the sun. Over the summer, the buds grow into plants, multiplying and providing food. In the fall, the cycle is completed when the vegetation dies and fertilizes the earth—providing nutrients for the next spring's buds. Expressed in a line, this scenario would seem final and maybe even tragic, but as a spiral there is security in knowing that what dies in the fall provides for new growth in the spring.

Spinning and life span

Later, in Greek mythology, the concept of the life cycle became more linear. Spinning was used metaphorically to describe the allotment of a person's life span through the myth of the Fates—the three sisters who spun,

Jacob
Norwegian-style Mittens
Alice Gillespie
Pennsylvania

measured, and cut the life thread of each mortal. They were considered more powerful than Zeus. The powerful trinity was feared by the ancient Greeks because this trio could arbitrarily decide the course of each human's life, and no other deity was believed to have the power to intervene. The maiden sister, Clotho, spun the golden thread of life, presiding over each mortal's birth. Her matron sister, Lachesis, measured the length of the thread and sometimes wove it into the cloth of destiny. It was the crone sister, Atropos, who cut the thread, ending life. The cyclical nature of human life and the seasons of the earth were personified in the myth of the Fates as they created human life through spinning. The circular motion of the spindle reiterated the circular motion of birth, life, and death.

The art of saving the sheep

While the objects in this exhibit don't claim to determine life spans, they do have subtle power. The spinners who contributed to the Save the Sheep project were interested in joining in a cycle that can help to ensure the conservation of endangered breeds of sheep. They became a part of the expanding spiral of conservation when they sought the fleece to make their garments. By demonstrating the diverse characteristics of the wool, they have generated excitement for conserving the breeds of sheep.

But these pieces go beyond giving a visible voice to the crusade to save the sheep. Finely crafted, these pieces are examples of ingenuity and

Jacob
Scarf of Many Colors
Suzanne Jones
Missouri

creativity—they hover between making things for practical purpose and expressing thoughts, feelings, and ideas. Each garment started as an idea and an entangled mass of fiber that needed to be sheared from the sheep, washed, dyed, combed or carded, and spun into yarn. Then the yarn had to be plied, and finally woven, knitted, or otherwise transformed into a design. An object which has been through these intimate processes has a powerful presence, whether it is worn or adorns a wall.

While most of these pieces were not intended to be art objects, they all possess many of the qualities we expect in artwork. They are beautiful and thought-provoking—they appeal to our aesthetic sense. These pieces ask us to think about the process of making. A yarn is spun and made into a garment—it is an unassuming process—and yet collectively these pieces have a voice. In their careful construction and compelling texture, they express opinions about sheep breeds that are in danger of extinction.

These spinners have created objects of subtle beauty and awe-inspiring craftsmanship—and more than that, their beliefs are caught up in the yarns.

Amy C. Clarke created her master's thesis exhibit from her own handspun yarn, which she knitted into a lot of socks, all of which were unpractical and fanciful. Fascinated by folklore, fairy tales, and mythology, she works out her visions in yarn and beads when she isn't providing editorial guidance for Beadwork *and* Spin-Off *magazines. She has recently become the editor of* Spin-Off.

right
Cotswold
Lace Shawl (on needles)
Debi Lee
Tennessee

In knitted lace, the work proceeds stitch by stitch and the pattern becomes clear after blocking.

far right
Lincoln Longwool
Fan-stitch Half-circle Shawl
Pat Noah
Colorado

> When we work on something so intimately for so long, it becomes part of us—and we, in turn, are held in the fabric of our creation.
>
> *Liz Johnson*
> *Utah*

Gute
Ewe and lambs. Photo by Barbro Ejendal, with thanks also to Ragnar Edberg and The Gute Sheep Society (Gutefårets hemsida).

Jurors

Jane Fournier
   spinner & co-author of *In Sheep's Clothing: A Handspinner's Guide to Wool*
Martha Hibberd
   co-owner, Hibberd McGrath Gallery, Breckenridge, Colorado
Terry McGrath Craig
   co-owner, Hibberd McGrath Gallery, Breckenridge, Colorado
Deborah Robson
   spinner, writer, visual artist, & editor of *Spin-Off* magazine

Note on the jurying

The work in the traveling exhibit was selected both to demonstrate some of what can be done with wools from endangered breeds and to make a coherent, diverse statement which will interest casual and experienced visitors to the show. Ten breeds are represented (alphabetically, with numbers of pieces): California Variegated Mutant/Romeldale (3); Cotswold (4); Jacob (1); Karakul (2); Manx Loghtan (1); Navajo Churro (7); Pitt Island Merino (1); Shetland (7); Tunis (1); Wensleydale (3).

The judges realized that Shetland and Navajo Churro are disproportionately represented. Both the quality and quantities of the work submitted in these wools undoubtedly reflect the success of recent conservation efforts, along with spinners' greater access to and familiarity with these particular fibers.

In this book, we have included work made of wool from eighteen additional breeds, for a total of twenty-eight (some in token appearances). Twenty-one of these are featured with breed notes (pages 52–70). Because of space constraints, we weren't able to offer information on the many other sheep breeds which are currently endangered.

This Save the Sheep project is a starting point, not a conclusion. At the end of a long, careful, productive day of evaluation and discussion, more than one of the jurors said, "What if there were another show of this type in a few years?"

It's an excellent question.

Deborah Robson

THE EXHIBIT

This exhibit presents works of art and craft created by contemporary hand-spinners from wool produced by rare and endangered breeds of sheep.

Both the skills of handspinning and the unique materials seem anachronistic. On the contrary, they embody irreplaceable foundations of human civilization. Machines can't do this quality of work. Chemistry, or even reverse biological engineering, can't replicate these fibers.

Very little is required to conserve these resources for the future: we need to pay attention and we need to spend some time. We need to acknowledge their importance.

The process starts here, as you simply enjoy what can happen when a sheep grows wool, a shepherd ensures the health and quality of the sheep, and then a spinner makes yarn which becomes a useful or fanciful object which enhances life.

Welcome.

Save the Sheep

The art of

endangered resources

Sheep and people formed a partnership for mutual survival long before many other components of what we consider human culture were discovered. Our primary concern in this exhibit is with wool and textiles, although sheep can provide all the essential elements of a good, if basic, life for humans: food, shelter, and clothing. Siberian houses called *yurts* are made of wool. Feta cheese and yogurt can be made from sheep's milk. Wool clothing encompasses options ranging from luxurious to rugged.

Humans first began using wool by collecting shed fibers. Primitive sheep can look out for themselves, don't need to be shorn, and produce two layers of wool in a single fleece. One layer consists of coarse fibers, which can be used to make durable fabrics, ropes, and other sturdy items. The second layer consists of fine fibers, better suited to soft textiles, like clothing.

The wide range of applications between coarse fibers (which are durable) and fine fibers (which are soft) appears dramatically in the work you see here. If the sweaters were made of coarse fibers, they would be so itchy (even scratchy) that no one could wear them. If the rugs were made of fine fibers, they would soon show signs of wear. Made from the appropriate types of wool, all of the handmade items you see here should last—and look good, in some cases even better—for many years.

◆

Breeds of sheep developed through close interactions between human needs, the sheep's genetic potential, and particular landscapes. Sheep adapted locally to climate and culture. Some developed the ability to survive in deserts, with minimal vegetation to eat. Other types withstand high temperatures while still growing wool coats, or tolerate areas of high rainfall. One particular breed, the North Ronaldsay, learned to thrive in the intertidal area of an island in the North Sea by eating seaweed.

Partnerships

Sheep

◆

Humans

◆

Landscape

◆

History

Contemporary agriculture in North America favors large sheep which produce quantities of meat. Wool is considered a "second crop," and most sheep raised on this continent produce a medium-grade wool which cannot even remotely perform the tasks of finer or coarser wools. It makes shabby rugs and hair-shirt underwear. Machine-processing transforms this medium-grade wool into adequate, but not superior, sweaters and coats.

Increasing dependence on mechanical, large-scale processing and the pressures of human population have marginalized the breeds of sheep whose wool you see here. These breeds may not produce large quantities of fiber or meat. They do produce fiber and meat at a very low ecological and economic cost.

They are *thrifty,* which means the right sheep in the right place can live well while promoting the health of the environment. They are *hardy,* which means they can withstand extremes of weather. They are *disease-resistant,* and they take care of their own young. None of these qualities can be taken for granted. A severe drought on the Navajo Nation a few years ago hit the region's more "modern" sheep hard, while the few Navajo Churro herds that have been re-established came through far better.

The right sheep can reclaim a landscape. While overgrazing can be a serious environmental threat resulting in erosion and desertification, several rare breeds, like Hebridean sheep and, again, Navajo Churros, are being used to control invasive scrub and weeds. Sheep can provide organic pest control on Christmas tree farms and in macadamia nut production, and can control summer vegetation growth on ski runs.

Breeds can die out quickly, taking with them resources we may never be able to reclaim. The wild mouflon, ancestor of modern sheep, grew fibers *twice as fine* as Merino, the contemporary standard of fine, soft wool. In 1920, there were 27,000 Oxford Down ewes. By 1970, there were less than 1,000—qualification for "endangered" status.

Cloning offers many fascinating possibilities for the future, but it won't preserve the genetic resources of these distinctive breeds. For that, we need viable, healthy, breeding populations large enough to avoid the hazards of inbreeding.

For handspinners, the range of fiber types available only from rare breeds provides the possibility of exchanging a bit of labor for a lot of luxury. On our floors, we put Navajo Churro rugs that are polished, more than worn, by passing generations of feet. We wrap our babies in soft Shetland blankets. We fend off the wind with Karakul.

We honor the past with the work of our hands. We conserve skills and resources for our children's benefit. We would like the world to be richer, not poorer, in the future.

We do this in partnership with sheep and the land.

As humans have, for many millennia.

Black Wensleydale
Photo courtesy of Upper Mill Farm, East Sussex, United Kingdom, and of Elite Genetics, Waukon, Iowa.

Navajo Churro
Dibé b'iiná' (Sheep is Life)
Lena Benally
Keams Canyon, Arizona
description on page 73

Wensleydale
Bobble-cuffed Socks
Jeannine Bakriges
Brattleboro, Vermont
description on page 73

Tunis
One fleece = one sheep = Tunis!
Johanna Bolton
Brooksville, Florida
description on page 74

Cotswold
Knitted and Felted Hat
Margaret Boos
Montague, California
description on page 74

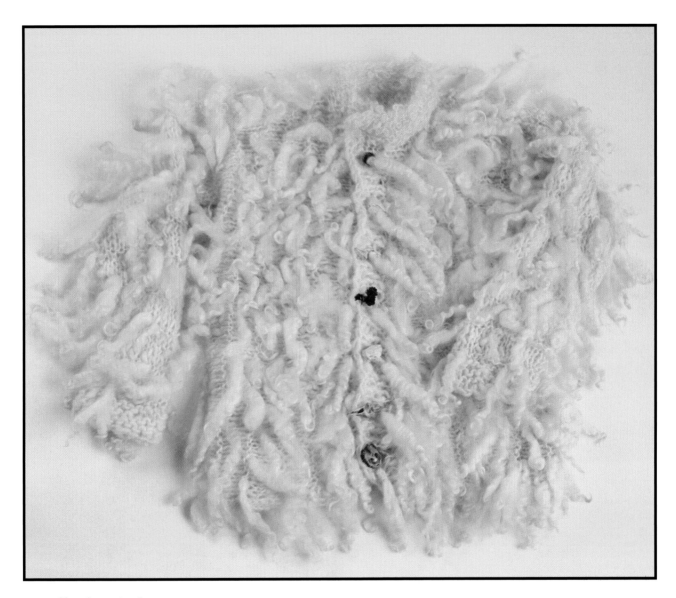

Cotswold and Navajo Churro
Cotswold Lock Jacket

Laurie Boyer
Orangeville, Illinois

description on page 74

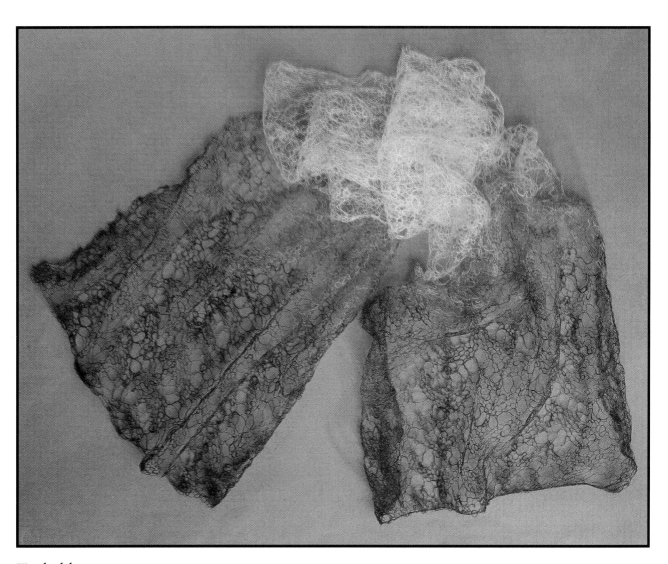

Wensleydale
Scarf
Brenda Bryon
East Sussex, United Kingdom
description on page 74

California Variegated Mutant
"Coming Home" Shawl
Kaye Collins
Fort Collins, Colorado
description on page 75

Navajo Churro
Churro Hat
Laurie Boyer
Orangeville, Illinois
description on page 75

Shetland
Flock
Teresa Gardner
Adrian, Missouri
description on page 75

Navajo Churro
Macramé Change Purse
and Round Mat
Mary Ellen ("Melon") Corsini
and Diane Ballerino-Regan
Supply, North Carolina
description on page 75

**Cotswold
Lace Blanket**
Jackie
Erickson-Schweitzer
Destrehan, Louisiana
description on page 76

Navajo Churro, Spelsau, Karakul, and Gotland
Window to the Past . . .
View of the Future?
Priscilla Gibson-Roberts
Cedaredge, Colorado
description on page 76

Wensleydale
Scarf
Suzi Gough
APO/United Kingdom
description on page 76

Shetland
Swedish-inspired Sweater
Greater Birmingham
Fiber Guild
Birmingham, Alabama
description on page 76

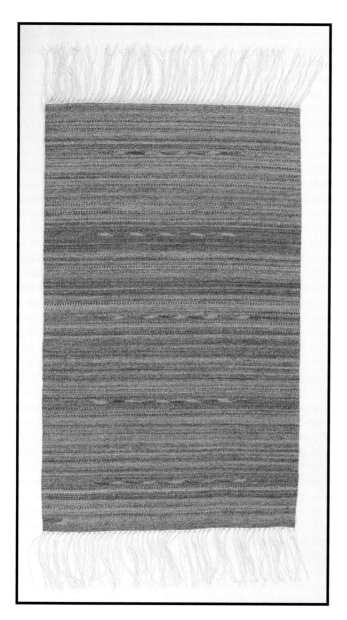

Shetland
Ragg Socks
Catherine Lampman
Hendersonville, Tennessee
description on page 77

Navajo Churro
Ojas del Otoño
Rita Padilla Haufmann
Tesuque, New Mexico
description on page 76

Pitt Island Merino
A Shawl for Great-Grandmother

Betty Kelly
Dunedin, New Zealand

description on page 77

Manx Loghtan
Scarf and Cap

Heather Maxey
Mayne, British Columbia, Canada

description on page 77

Shetland
Scarf

Joanne Littler
Fairfax, Vermont
description on page 77

California Variegated Mutant
Socks

Jan Viren
Hastings, Minnesota
description on page 77

Shetland
Sunset Kimono
Sara Lamb
Colfax, California
description on page 78

Shetland
Fair Isle Coat

Shetland Guild of Spinners, Weavers, and Dyers
Shetland Islands, Scotland
description on page 78

Cotswold
Vest
Robin Metzger
Corvallis, Oregon
description on page 78

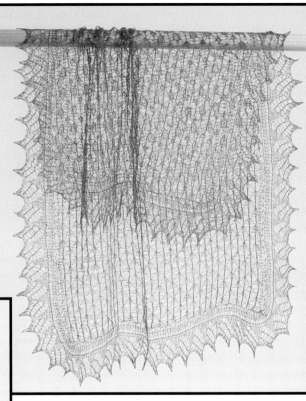

Shetland
Lace Scarf
Anne Silk
Prince Edward Island, Canada
description on page 78

California Variegated Mutant
Byzantine Vest
Sarah Swett
Moscow, Idaho
description on page 78

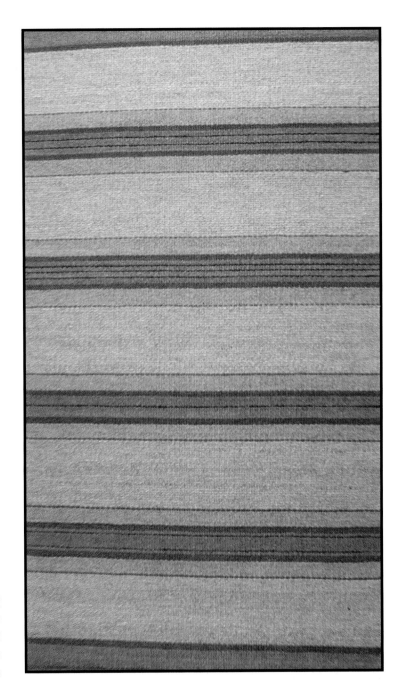

Karakul
Red Karakul Rug
Barbara Kent Stafford
Napa, California
description on page 78

Jacob
Colleen's Coat
Mary Underwood and
Rebecca Lambers
Ann Arbor, Michigan
description on page 79

Navajo Churro
Turtledove in Red
Ellen Sullivan
Valley Center, California
description on page 79

A SAMPLING OF SHEEP

The breeds listed here are featured in this book. A complete list of breeds considered rare by The American Livestock Breeds Conservancy (North America) and the Rare Breeds Survival Trust (United Kingdom) at the time of the Save the Sheep project appears on page 19. The numbers in parentheses within the text cross-reference pages where you can see other pieces made of a given type of wool.

California Variegated Mutant & Romeldale

California Variegated Mutant
Photo courtesy of Lewis White and
The American Livestock Breeds Conservancy.

CVM/Romeldale
Cyclone Vest
Diane Ballerino-Regan
North Carolina

Developed in the twentieth century in California, the Romeldale and California Variegated Mutant (CVM) can be considered either two closely related breeds or the white and multicolored variants of one breed. These sheep grow fine, soft wool in large quantities. For years, the entire clip of the original Romeldale flock was sold to Pendleton Mills.

Breeding for the California Variegated Mutant, in particular, has emphasized spinnability of the fiber, with a focus on handspinners, who are the dominant market for all natural-colored wool. As a bonus, the fiber comes in white, gray, black, and brown, often with multiple shades grown by a single animal. Kaye Collins, who made her "Coming Home" Shawl from CVM, says, "I chose this fleece strictly because of the unusually rich brown color, which reminded me of the earth."

Annually, each sheep grows 8–15 pounds (3.5–6.8 kg) of wool, or enough for between five and eight sweaters. Staple lengths average 4–6 inches (10–15 cm), and counts run 60s–62s, or a little finer.

Items in this book made of California Variegated Mutant or Romeldale wool: Diane Ballerino-Regan, vest (this page); Diane Bentley-Baker, shawl (12); Kaye Collins, shawl (37); Phyllis Karsten, christening shawl (25); Jacquie Kelly, shawl (12); Robin Lynde, socks (12); Sarah Swett, vest (48); Jan Viren, socks (44).

Cotswold

Cotswolds hail from the hills of western England. Their ancestors may have been in that area for more than 2000 years—since the time of Caesar. They're named for the *cots,* in which the sheep sheltered for the night, and the *wolds,* the treeless, hilly, not very fertile land they roamed during the day. For hundreds of years, these sheep supported a robust regional economy. They've found contemporary homes in living-history farms, abbeys, and other community, as well as private, conservation efforts.

Cotswolds' very long locks measure 6–12 inches (15–30 cm), and each sheep produces enough fiber in a year to make three or four sturdy jacket-type sweaters—about 9–15 pounds (4–6.8 kg), with a count of 38s–48s.

Although most Cotswolds grow white wool, breeders today are working to foster the breed's color

Cotswolds
On left, April, a ewe; on right, King Lear, a ram. Photo courtesy of Anne Williams.

possibilities, which mostly run to blacks. The golden gray in Jackie Erickson-Schweitzer's "Lace Blanket" is an extraordinary color for any breed (page 39), although

its shine, smooth surface, body, and elegant drape say *Cotswold* all over.

Items in this book made of Cotswold: Margaret Boos, hat (34); Laurie Boyer, jacket (35); Jackie Erickson-Schweitzer, blanket (39); The Homeplace 1850 collection of wristwarmers, scarf, and hat by Jackie Cravens, Cindy Earls, and Amanda Nikkel (23); Susan Anne Metz, shawl (this page); Robin Metzger, vest (47); Noreen Muellerweiss, mittens (4) and socks (24); Catherine Reimers and Nancy Bertino, dog lead (4); the Tri-Community Adult Education Weaving and Spinning Class of Covina, California, vest (this page); Anne Williams, hat (10).

right
Cotswold
Seamus' Vest
Tri-Community Adult Education
Weaving and Spinning Class
Covina, California

far right
Cotswold
Shawl
Susan Anne Metz
Missouri

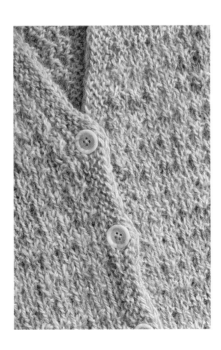

Dorset Horn

The Dorset Horn has ancient origins in southwestern England and is also associated with most of Wales. It is considered one of the oldest English breeds and produces one of the highest-quality English wools. Both rams and ewes have horns—the rams' horns are longer, heavier, and more emphatically curved. Dorset Horns were imported into the United States about 1860. Dorset Polls began through a genetic mutation that occurred in the early 1950s. Both breeds can lamb twice a year and tolerate heat well.

Dorset Horns' Down-type fleece is "remarkably white even before scouring,"[1] strong, dense, matte-surfaced, crisp, and free from dark fiber. The staple length is 2½–4 inches (6–10 cm), and a ewe can produce 4½–6½ pounds (2–3 kg) of wool a year. Counts average 46s–58s, with most falling between 50s and 56s (32–27 microns).

Items in this book made of Dorset Horn: Frances Irving, socks (this page); Martha Williams, socks, which incorporate Shetland patterning as well (this page).

[1] Skinner, Lord, and Williams, *British Sheep and Wool*, page 43.

Dorset Horn
Photo courtesy of Frances Irving.

> *Note:* There are three types of sheep called Dorset. Two are closely related and have white faces: the **Dorset Horn**, which is rare, and the **Dorset Poll**, developed from the Dorset Horn, which is very common.
> **Dorset Downs**, unrelated to both Dorset Horns and Dorset Polls, have brown faces and feet.

far left
Dorset Horn

Socks

Frances Irving
Manitoba, Canada

left
Dorset Horn
with Shetland patterning

Socks

Martha Williams
Iowa

Gulf Coast Native

Spanish explorers and settlers brought sheep to North America beginning in the 1500s, and established primary flocks in the Southwest and the Southeast. Gulf Coast Native sheep represent the Southeastern contingent, able to withstand heat and humidity, and to resist footrot, internal parasites, and other maladies prevalent in warm, moist locales.[1]

For many years, these were the only sheep to be found in the deep South. They don't require intensive management because they are so well adapted to their surroundings, and they lamb year-round. A group of Gulf Coast sheep was recently acquired by the Disney Animal Kingdom, because of their ability to tolerate the Florida climate.

The Gulf Coast Native's fine wool suggests origins in Merino-type genetics, as well as Churro forebears. Most sheep of this type are white, but fleece colors range through tans to dark brown, occasionally to black. Some animals have spotted faces and legs. The wool has a staple length of 2½–4 inches (6–10 cm), with a count of 48s–58s, micron measurements of 32–26, and annual fleece weights of 4–6 pounds (1.75–2.75 kg).

Items in this book made of Gulf Coast Native wool: Maureen Burnett, slipper socks (this page); Patricia Piehota, vest (this page).

[1] *Navajo Churro sheep, developed from similar introductions into the Southwest, adapted to aridity and sparse vegetation.*

Gulf Coast Native
Photo courtesy of Patricia Piehota, Gulf Coast Breeders Association, Oklahoma.

right
Gulf Coast Native
Aran-patterned Vest
Patricia Piehota
Oklahoma

far right
Gulf Coast Native
Helen's Slipper Socks
Maureen Burnett
Mississippi

Hog Island

About two hundred years ago, Hog Island sheep developed as a feral, or wild, breed on a barrier island near the mouth of the James River in Virginia. Their origins trace to local sheep with British roots, and they are believed to have a lot of Merino blood. A similarly wild group became well established off the coast of California, as Santa Cruz sheep.

In 1974, The Nature Conservancy bought Hog Island, and subsequently removed the entire sheep population. The genetic resource which these animals represent is being maintained in flocks elsewhere. Gunston Hall Plantation, in Fairfax County, Virginia, currently uses a small flock of Hog Island sheep in a living-history presentation of eighteenth-century life.

Hog Islands possess extraordinary hardiness, foraging ability, and reproductive efficiency, having survived for centuries in an extremely harsh environment, with a limited diet and no medical attention. They may be useful in the future for grassland maintenance or conservation.

Most Hog Island sheep are white, although about 10 percent are black. Both ewes and rams can be horned. They grow a medium-weight wool, producing about 3½–5 pounds (1.5–2.25 kg) a year.

Items in this book made of Hog Island wool: Gail Johnson, slipper socks (this page); Sara Gene Posnett, shawl (this page).

Hog Island
Ram, Accokeek, Maryland. Photo courtesy of Sara Gene Posnett.

left
Hog Island
Slipper Socks
Gail Johnson
Minnesota

right
Hog Island
Sunston Shawl
Sara Gene Posnett
Pennsylvania

Jacob (American)

Here's a puzzler. The Jacob sheep found in North America are endangered, while those found in the United Kingdom are not. How come? Jacobs in the United Kingdom have been "improved" to produce bigger sheep that give more meat. North American Jacobs retain the breed's ancient characteristics, resembling the sheep shown in Egyptian paintings (1800 B.C.E.), Scythian gold work (1000 B.C.E.), and Sicilian pottery (600 B.C.E.).

Even an amateur can pick out the Jacobs in the crowd. There are very few other spotted sheep (Harlequins come to mind), but no other breed has coloring quite as dramatic as Jacobs'—or those horns, found on both ewes and rams. These sheep may have two, four, or even six horns, and you can tell the ewes because they have the more delicate sets of head ornaments. Each sheep grows two colors of wool—white and a second color, most often black but sometimes brownish, or a lighter color called *lilac*. Breeders tend to like Jacobs' personalities (curious and intelligent), and be amused (sometimes confounded) by their agility. Jacobs produce relatively small fleeces (about enough for a sweater and a matching hat and pair of mittens each year), but with those colors in a nice, sturdy wool, who cares?

Fleece weights average 3–6 pounds (1.3–2.7 kg), with staple lengths of 3–6 inches (8–15 cm) and counts of 48s–56s (33–26 microns).

Items in this book made of Jacob wool: Joan Berner and Linda Geiger, throw (5); Alice Gillespie, mittens (28); Suzanne Jones, scarf (28); the Manitoba Handspinners, afghan (this page); Mary Underwood and Rebecca Lambers, jacket (50).

Jacob
Four-month-old, four-horned ewe lamb.
Photo courtesy of Mary Spahr,
Spahr Farm, Ohio.

Jacob
Afghan
Manitoba Handspinners
Manitoba, Canada

Karakul

Several rare breeds vie for the title of "oldest breed of domesticated sheep," and the Karakul is one of these. Carvings that look like Karakuls can be found on ancient Babylonian temples, and the breed's name comes from the Bokhara region, near the Caspian and Black Seas—a place of high altitude with scant, desert vegetation and little water.

Like the Jacob, it's the American version of Karakul that's endangered. Introduced to the United States in the early twentieth century,

Karakuls
Ewe and lamb. Photo courtesy of Jeffrey Black, East Central University, Ada, Oklahoma, and The American Livestock Breeds Conservancy.

these sheep thrive under adverse conditions and can live on marginal land that would not support ordinary sheep. The lifespan of many sheep is determined by their teeth, which wear out from grazing. Karakuls have very strong teeth, which enhances their ability to live a long time. They're also likely to fight dogs who try to herd them. Karakuls are unusual because their gene for black fleece is dominant. Lambs are born black. As they mature, their fleeces may stay that color (called *arabi*) or shift to a variety of other strong colors— *guligas* (rosy), *kambar* (brown), *shirazi* (gray), *agouti* (mixed light and dark)—as well as off-white, silver-gray, and golden tan. The wool grows as a long, strong, lustrous outer coat and a fine, soft inner coat, which can be used separately or in combination.

Fleece weights average 2½–10 pounds (1–4.5 kg), with staple lengths of 6–12 inches (15–30 cm), and counts of 50s or coarser (29 or more microns).

Items in this book made of Karakul wool: the mini-skeins in Priscilla Gibson-Roberts' work (40); Marjorie Mills, "Barn Angel" (this page); Peggy Siders, bag (this page); Barbara Kent Stafford, rug (49).

Karakul
Karakul Bag
Peggy Siders
Indiana

Karakul
Barn Angel
Marjorie Mills
Michigan

Leicester Longwool

Colonial Williamsburg chose Leicester Longwools for its interpretation and breeding program. As shepherd Elaine Shirley says, "Colonial Williamsburg could easily display any breed of sheep and most people would not know the difference." Yet the foundation decided not only to display but to work hard for the conservation of a delightful breed developed in England during the 1700s as part of the first modern breeding program. George Washington used Leicester bloodlines in his flock at Mount Vernon.

Also called English Leicester (the distinctive word is pronounced *lester*), these animals provided the foundation for many

Leicester Longwools
Ewe and lambs. Photo courtesy of
Colonial Williamsburg Foundation.

modern breeds. Fewer than two hundred North American registrations occur annually, placing them on the critical list for conservation. Medium to large in size, Leicesters produce lots of wool—11–20 pounds per animal per year. The

long, lustrous, spiraling fibers give body, character, and durability to woven and knitted fabrics. Machine-processed Leicester wool which we've seen doesn't speak well for its exquisite qualities; it tends to become dull, limp, and uninspiring. However, attentive handspinners can turn this fleece into shining fabrics with excellent drape and texture.

Fleece weights average 11–15 pounds, sometimes up to 20 pounds (5–6.8 kg, up to 9 kg), with staple lengths of 8–10 inches (20–25 cm) and counts of 40s–46s (38–32 microns).

Item in this book made of Leicester Longwool: Rae Jean Rimmer, shawl (this page).

right & far right
Leicester Longwool

Raspberries-and-Cream

Wrap

Rae Jean Rimmer
Virginia

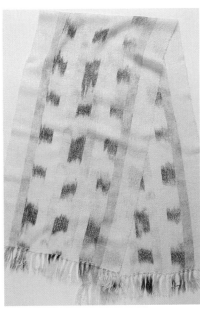

Lincoln Longwool

Lincoln Longwool
Six-month-old ewe lamb.
Photo courtesy of Roger Watkins, Lincoln Association, Mt. Horeb, Wisconsin.

Lincolns are big—they're often called the world's largest breed of sheep. Mature rams weigh 250–350 pounds (113–159 kg), and ewes 200–250 pounds (91–113 kg). Lincolns have also been around a long time; their ancestors may have been brought to Britain by the Romans. Adapted to harsh climates, they first crossed the Atlantic to North America after the Revolutionary War. Lincolns have been used in the development of breeds throughout the world.

In addition to pure body mass, they grow proportionately huge quantities of strong, high-quality wool, carried in heavy locks that twist into spirals and have significant luster. The fiber's staple length is among the longest of all breeds, usually measuring 7–15 inches (17.5–38 cm), although one ewe grew wool almost 32 inches (81 cm) long. There's lots of it, too. Ewes produce 12–20 pounds (5.5–9 kg), and one ram grew a fleece weighing over 46 pounds (21 kg) in one year. These are record-setting, although even the average production lengths and weights—easier to handle—are impressive. Most Lincoln wool arrives in fleece-weights of 12–15 pounds (5.5–7 kg), with staple lengths of 7–10 inches (17.5–25 cm), with counts on the fine end of 36s–46s (41–33.5 microns). That's hefty.

Items in this book made of Lincoln wool: Dobree Adams, "Wild Asters" (this page); Pat Noah, shawl (29).

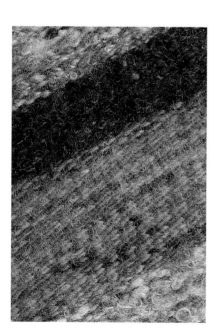

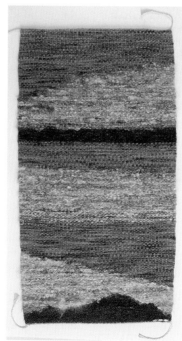

left & center
Lincoln Longwool
Wild Asters
Dobree Adams
Kentucky

Manx Loghtan

Manx Loghtan sheep may be descended from ancestors the Vikings brought to the Isle of Man and used as part of their supply line for raids in the area. They're both hardy and thrifty, which means they can survive on low levels of nutrition. A hundred years ago, there were black and white Manx sheep, as well as the brown which remains today.

In the late nineteenth century one person, John Caesar Bacon, saved the breed from extinction. There are a thousand or fewer Manx sheep today. They're easy to manage and, like Karakuls, have strong teeth which support their ability to live a long time. Manx ewes are about the size of Labrador Retrievers; the rams are larger. Each sheep produces 3½–4½ pounds (1.5–2 kg) of fleece a year, or enough for a small family's caps and mittens.

Staple lengths average 2¾–4 inches (7–10 cm), with counts of 44s–54s.

Items in this book made of Manx Loghtan wool: Heather Maxey, scarf and cap (43); Edna Smith, vest (this page).

Manx Loghtans
Photo courtesy of Sue Gotting.

left & right
Manx Loghtan

Vest

Edna Smith
Alberta, Canada

Navajo Churro

Navajo Churro sheep, well established in the Southwestern United States for the better part of four hundred years, have nearly slipped into extinction several times, although their situation looks better today than it has in 150 years. Descended from the first domesticated sheep in the New World, they form the foundation for the Rio Grande, Pueblo, and Navajo textile traditions.

Navajo Churro fleece displays luster, a silky feel, many natural colors, and astounding durability. Well-woven rugs of this wool look better after fifty years of wear, and old textiles woven with it possess an incomparable integrity and presence. In the 1860s, the United States government nearly destroyed all the native sheep in an attempt to control the Navajo people. In the late nineteenth and early twentieth centuries, well-intended but misguided efforts to "improve" the breed almost extinguished it, and in the 1930s attempts to control rangeland erosion—which had accelerated with increased numbers of crossbred sheep—almost destroyed the breed entirely. Only a few survivors remained, in isolated villages and remote canyons. In the

Navajo Churros
Ewe and lambs. Photo courtesy of Tonya Charter and The American Livestock Breeds Conservancy.

Navajo Churro
Scarf #3
Connie Taylor
New Mexico

1970s, a few people began to retrieve and breed the remaining animals. These sheep can withstand hot dry deserts and subzero conditions, and produce wool in white, silver, blue-gray, brown, red, and black. As with many of the so-called primitive breeds, their grazing habits are being shown to facilitate the restoration of grasslands and fragile ecosystems.

Fleece weights average 4–7 pounds (1.8–3.2 kg). The outer coat averages 4–14 inches (10–35 cm) in length, with counts up to 36s (38 microns and coarser). The inner coat averages 2–4 inches (5–10 cm) in length, with counts around 62s (23–22 microns).

Items in this book made of Navajo Churro wool: Lena Benally, *Dibé b'iiná'* (33); Laurie Boyer, hat (37); Melon Corsini and Diane Ballerino-Regan, change purse and round mat (38); the miniature pair of Iranian stockings and the wool on the spindle in Priscilla Gibson-Roberts' work (40); Rita Padilla Haufmann, *Ojas del Otoño* (42); Kathrin Olson-Rutz, shawl (16); D. Phillip Sponenberg, vest (detail, 16); Ellen Sullivan, rug (51); Connie Taylor, scarf (this page).

North Ronaldsay

These extremely hardy sheep live on the shore of the northernmost of the Orkney Islands, off the northeast coast of Scotland, where they thrive on a diet of seaweed. The sheep do select the best and juiciest seaweed. They've been living in the intertidal area since at least 1832. They're capable of surviving harsh conditions, and have been described as an animal "which knows the ebb and flow of the sea as accurately as any . . . tide table" (Peter Tulloch). Changes in their physiology and behavior have resulted from their unusual environment. They cannot be worked by dogs, and the ewes protect their lambs from predatory seabirds.

Believed to represent Iron-Age domestic sheep, North Ronaldsays come in a range of colors, from pure white through tans, grays, and browns, to black. However, the fleece mixes coarse and fine fibers and often the color appears to be carried in the coarse fibers, over a white or off-white array of fine wool. In the true black and true white fleeces, both coarse and fine fibers are black or white. Each sheep grows $3\frac{1}{2}$–$5\frac{1}{2}$ pounds (1.5–2.5 kg) of wool a year, with a staple length of $1\frac{1}{2}$–3 inches (4–8 cm) and a count of 50s–56s (31–26 microns).

Items in this book made of North Ronaldsay wool: Danette Pratt, sock (this page); Deborah Pulliam, socks (this page).

North Ronaldsays
Rams. Photo courtesy of Brian Cassie, Hon. Secretary, The North Ronaldsay Fellowship, Leicestershire, United Kingdom.

North Ronaldsay
Sock
Danette Pratt
Ohio

left & center
North Ronaldsay
Socks
Deborah Pulliam
Maine

Pitt Island

When the sun rises on each new year, its earliest beams touch the Chatham Islands, just west of the International Date Line. A group of sheep lives here that was delivered to one island in 1860, then abandoned. Sheep who survive abandonment become feral, or wild, and the only ones who live and breed are those that can take care of themselves.

Few feral groups come as directly from fine-wool genetics as these Pitt Islands. Most feral sheep are either primitive (not far removed from the survival traits of early sheep) or medium-fibered. Wild sheep come with, or develop, the

Pitt Islands
Photo courtesy of Betty Kelly.

ability to shed their wool. Cultivated sheep require human intervention in the form of shearing. Selection on Pitt Island favored

sheep with camouflage, so the animals grow wool in a variety of colors—very unusual for Merino-based stock. The wool they produce is also structurally unique. In addition to the usual wave pattern, or crimp, the fibers have a corkscrew formation. From their relaxed state, they can be stretched almost double in length. This is astounding, and permits the spinning of extraordinarily elastic yarns.

Fleeces average 4½ pounds (2 kg), with staple lengths of 2¼–3½ inches (5.7–9 cm).

Item in this book made of Pitt Island wool: Betty Kelly, shawl (43).

Ryeland

Famous for more than six centuries, the Ryeland originated in the west of England. It is one of Britain's oldest breeds and has always produced very high-quality wool. In fact, it's said to have been "renowned in Elizabethan times for its golden fleece of the highest quality."[1] Hornless, fertile, and heavy-milking, the Ryeland has adapted to many types of pastures throughout the world and, in combination with the Dorset Horn, contributed to development of the common Dorset Poll.

Ryeland's Down-type wool is soft, light, springy, and clear white.

Each sheep produces 5–9 pounds (2.25–4 kg) of wool per year, with a staple length of 3–6 inches (7.5–15 cm) and a count of 50s–58s, mostly on the finer end (32–26 microns).

Items in this book made of Ryeland wool: Sammie Oaks, miniature sock; Martha Williams, mittens (both, this page).

[1] Richard Lutwyche, "From Sheep to Shawl: A look at the Natural Fibre Company," page 60. The "famous for more than six centuries" statement comes from Skinner, Lord, and Williams, *British Sheep and Wool*, page 88.

Santa Cruz Island

Santa Cruz Island
Elsa, the ewe who grew the wool for Nancy Van Tassel's shawl. Photo courtesy of Nancy Van Tassel.

These feral sheep were abandoned on Santa Cruz Island, one of the Channel Islands off the coast of California, somewhere between 70 and 200 years ago. They overgrazed their limited environment, and when The Nature Conservancy acquired ownership of the island in 1978 the organization began to eradicate the sheep in order to restore habitats for wildlife species.

opposite

Ryeland
Miniature Stocking Ornament
Sammie Oaks
New Mexico

Ryeland
Mittens
Martha Williams
Iowa

Small and exceptionally hardy, Santa Cruz sheep thrive on minimal forage. They have virtually no birthing problems and a high survival rate. The American Livestock Breeds Conservancy, recognizing the genetic value of the sheep as well as the wildlife, began to collaborate with The Nature Conservancy on a rescue operation beginning in 1988. In that year, twelve lambs were moved off the island and placed with breeders to begin rebuilding the population in other locations.

Most Santa Cruz Island sheep are white, but they also come in black, brown, and spotted. The wool is fine to medium and very soft. It has a tendency to felt, is very elastic, and is short and fine enough to require some practice in the spinning.

Item in this book made of Santa Cruz Island wool: Nancy Van Tassel, shawl (detail, this page).

Santa Cruz Island
Wedding-ring Lace Shawl
Nancy Van Tassel
California

Feral sheep

Sheep rarely survive without human intervention, so feral, or wild, flocks around the world carry genes for unusually strong constitutions and instincts. Feral flocks most often succeed on islands with relatively few predators.

In North America, feral sheep breeds developed on Hog Island, off the East Coast, and Santa Cruz Island, off the West Coast. In both cases, these hardy sheep have been caught in the middle of a moral dilemma because they occupy habitats which have become important to the conservation of wild species. Human activities have consumed increasing amounts of land formerly used by wild, feral, and domesticated animals, placing wildlife conservation at odds with conservation of domesticated breeds, as well as general agriculture.

Shetland

Although Shetland sheep are on their way to becoming a conservation success story, their wonderful color genetics are still at risk, since most of the Shetland sheep on the mainland of the United Kingdom are white.

Shetlands have lived on a set of windswept islands between Scotland and Norway for more than a thousand years. A few Shetlands have been raised in North America since Thomas Jefferson kept some at Monticello. Recent interest in natural fibers and natural-colored clothing has increased support for breeders who tend these hardy, calm, intelligent sheep, which are about the size of large Labrador Retrievers and grow very fine, soft wool. The wool comes in eleven identified colors, from white through browns and grays to black.

Shetland
Ewe. Photo courtesy of Judi Lehrhaupt, Ewe Can Do It Sheep Farm, Newtown, Pennsylvania.

The colors have Gaelic names like *moorit, emsket, shaela,* and *mioget.* The people of the Shetland Islands use the wool to knit color-patterned garments (named Fair Isle, for one of the islands) and two types of traditional shawls: light-weight, lacy "ring" shawls (fine enough to pull through a wedding ring) and heavier, everyday shawls.

Fleece weights average 2–4 pounds (1–1.8 kg), with staple lengths of 2–5 inches (5–12 cm), with counts from the high 50s to low 60s (20–12 microns for inner coat and 40–30 microns for outer coat).

Items in this book made of Shetland wool: Vicki Ball, socks (this page); Jane Burton, scarf (74); Teresa Gardner, sweater (38); the Greater Birmingham Fiber Guild, sweater-jacket (41); Cynthia Heeren, shawl (74); Liz Johnson, vest (detail, 4); Sara Lamb, kimono (45); Catherine Lampman, socks (42); Judi Lehrhaupt, hat (this page); Joanne Littler, scarf (44); the Shetland Guild of Spinners, Weavers, and Dyers, coat (46); and Anne Silk, scarf (47).

Shetland
Gray Socks
Vicki Ball
Vermont

Shetland
Shepherd's Spiral
Judi Lehrhaupt
Pennsylvania

Shetland
My Shetland Flock Vest,
sample components
Joan Contraman
Montana

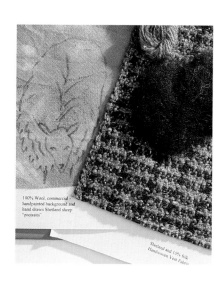

100% Wool, commercial handpainted background and hand drawn Shetland sheep "protraits"

Shetland and 10% Silk Handwoven Vest Fabric

Soay

These small, very primitive sheep inhabited the British Isles before the arrival of the Norse or Roman invaders—they probably arrived in northern Europe more than 4,000 years ago. They are believed to represent Bronze-Age domestic sheep. Most are now found on a set of islands quite a distance into the North Atlantic from the coast of Scotland. Soays, like other sheep which can survive with little or no human intervention, lack a flocking instinct and cannot be managed with sheep dogs. The males carry horns, as do some of the females.

Soays' fleece varies from light to dark brown, and they naturally shed the wool in the summer. The remarkably fine fleece can be

Soays
Rams at Bunstye Farm, Sussex, showing moulting of wool in summer. Photo courtesy of Michelle Green, West Sussex, United Kingdom.

variable. While the double coat contains finer and coarser fibers, the two types can be hard to differentiate. Annual production per animal averages 3–5 pounds of wool (1.25–2.25 kg), with a staple length of 2–6 inches (5–15 cm) and a count of 44s–50s (36–29 microns).

Sturdy, thrifty Soays have been useful in the reclamation of gravel pits and other low-fertility areas. Lawrence Alderson, the United Kingdom's recently retired expert on rare livestock breeds, made the following comment about Soays: "It is only since 1970 that a serious, objective evaluation of the breed has been made. The results are a devastating comment on 10,000 years of domestication and livestock improvement."[1]

Items in this book made of Soay wool: Barbara Ballas, scarf; Tan Summers, miniature helmet (both, this page).

[1] Lawrence Alderson, *The Chance to Survive*, page 61.

Soay
Miniature Moss-stitch Helmet
Tan Summers
Utah

Soay
Saint Kilda Scarf
Barbara Ballas
Oregon

Southdown

The Southdown is the original Down sheep, and for more than two hundred years it has grazed southern England and contributed to the development of all other Down breeds. It has the finest of the Down wools. Southdowns in the United Kingdom, New Zealand, and France represent the breed's original values. Southdowns in the United States have evolved into a breed which goes by the same name but has different qualities and is not endangered.

Southdowns are small to medium-sized and hornless. They mature early, lamb well, and adapt to varied and wet climates. Their wool is soft, elastic, and insulating, and grows in tight, thick staples. A year's growth of wool averages 3½–8 pounds (1.5–3.6 kg), with a staple length of 1½–3 inches (4–7.5 cm) and a count of 54s–60s (29–23 microns).

Item in this book made of Southdown wool: Veronica de Olive-Lowe, tiny sheep (this page).

Southdown
Tiny Sheep
Veronica de Olive-Lowe
New Zealand

Teeswater

Teeswaters are one of the largest and most ancient of the British longwool breeds, and are noted for prolificacy, sometimes producing four or five lambs at a time. They are often used in crosses for this reason, an action which emphasizes their value without ensuring their conservation. They are found in northern England, Wales, and the border region.

Teeswaters grow a heavy fleece of fine, long-stapled wool. Like Wensleydale, Teeswater wool is unusually fine for its length and fleece quality has been part of the breed's standard. A fleece averages 8–15 pounds (3.5–7 kg), with a staple length of 6–12 inches (15–30 cm) and a count of 40s–48s.

Item in this book made of Teeswater wool: Nanette Mosher, rug (4).

Teeswater
Photo courtesy of David W. Ward, The Teeswater Sheep Breeder's Association, North Yorkshire, United Kingdom.

Tunis

Tunis sheep trace their origins to North Africa. They appeared in North America in the late 1700s, making them one of the oldest breeds indigenous to this continent. Records kept by Thomas Jefferson, John Adams, and George Washington refer to these sheep. There were quite a few flocks established before the Civil War destroyed almost all of these animals.

Although the ancestors of Tunis sheep are believed to date to biblical times, at this point the breed is unique to North America. Jefferson preferred them to his Merinos. Tunis lambs are born red or tan. As they grow, the fleece turns creamy white while the faces, ears, and legs retain the rosy color. Over the past ten years, Tunis sheep have increased in numbers. They are calm, sturdy, disease-resistant, and able to make do on marginal land. They like heat and humidity, but can handle cold as well. Each sheep produces between six and nine pounds of relatively fine wool a year—enough to make between two and four sweaters, or a couple of cosy blankets.

Fleece weights average 6–12 pounds (2.7–5.4 kg), with staple lengths of 3–6 inches (7.6–15 cm) and counts of 56s–58s (30–24 microns).

Items in this book made of Tunis wool: Johanna Bolton, sheep (34); Sharon Schulz, mittens (this page).

Tunis
Ram lambs. Photo courtesy of Deborah Hunter-Simon, Shepherds of Goose Pass, Springport, Michigan, and The American Livestock Breeds Conservancy.

Tunis
Mittens with Angora Cuffs
Sharon Schulz
North Dakota

Wensleydale

Wensleydales grow large quantities of very long, fine, curly fleece. Most long-wool fleeces are coarse and contain fibers called kemp, which are stiff and scratchy. Wensleydales are entirely kemp-free. Their delicate, shiny fibers require—and reward—careful processing. Most Wensleydales grow white wool, although a recent breeding effort in the United Kingdom focuses on colored Wensleydales.

In the 1960s, only two hundred Wensleydale sheep remained and the breed nearly died out. If it had vanished, it's possible that no amount of retroactive breeding attempts could have reproduced the quality of wool that would have been disappeared with these sheep—in particular, the combina-

Black Wensleydales
Photo courtesy of Upper Mill Farm, East Sussex, United Kingdom, and of Elite Genetics, Waukon, Iowa.

tion of length, shine, softness, and colors. Humans appear to have already lost some of the genetic fiber potential in sheep. Merinos, currently the standard breed producing the finest wool, grow fibers that measure about 22.5 microns in diameter. Archaeological evidence from the Crimea shows that during the fifth century B.C.E. textiles were made with wool fibers that averaged only 15 microns in diameter. For comparison, cashmere (which is grown by goats) must measure less than 18.5 microns. Some wools are finer than this, but not many.

Even cloning offers a poor substitute for conservation of original breed types, since a clone by definition does not produce adequate genetic diversity to ensure a stable, healthy population of animals.

Fleece weights average 8–15 pounds (3.5–7 kg), with staple lengths of 8–12 inches (20–30 cm) and counts from 44s–48s (may be as fine as 30 microns).

Items in this book made of Wensleydale wool: Jeannine Bakriges, socks (33); Brenda Bryon, scarf (36); Suzi Gough, scarf (41); Marie Mercuri, mittens (this page).

Wensleydale

Mittens

Marie Mercuri
Illinois

TREASURES DESCRIBED

PAGE 4

Teeswater
Rug
Nanette Mosher, Illinois

Nanette Mosher maintains a flock of colored Cheviots for the valuable genetic work of preserving recessive colors in purebred sheep. For this project, she spun Teeswater top and wove a rug which demonstrates that very different wool's luster and affinity for color. The fabric is heavy, supple, and durable.

Cotswold
Mittens
Noreen Muellerweiss, Michigan

Noreen Muellerweiss has kept Cotswolds for almost twenty years. She says, "I have learned a little about animal husbandry, genetics, spinning, knitting, and weaving. But . . . the highlight of my experiences remains in daily care of my Cotswold flock and the placement of breeding stock." Noreen spun thin singles for mittens which show off Cotswold's shine. Noreen's sheep, at Stow-on-the-Wold, grew the wool Lena Benally used to spin the warp for her small rug on page 33.

Cotswold
Emerald City Dog Lead
Catherine Reimers & Nancy Bertino, New York

Catherine wrote, "This fanciful but practical item was an adventure. Nancy usually spins soft wools for garments and I, a knitter, have just begun to weave. I had a new inkle loom and she a new dog—a perfect match!" Cotswold

is an excellent choice. Shiny and durable, it takes color well. It's also smooth enough to feel comfortable in a dog-walker's hand.

Shetland
Fair Isle Vest
Liz Johnson, Utah

Liz Johnson dyed two-ply gray Shetland grown by Blue Mist at Yaquina View Farm, Oregon, with colors inspired by a David Muench photograph on a poster commemorating the Wilderness Act. She says, "The photograph shows alpine wildflowers and lichens, their vivid colors and fragile beauty contrasting with their rugged environment. I liked the fact that the poster was celebrating the American wilderness, another 'endangered breed.'" She also says, "When we work on something so intimately for so long, it becomes part of us—and we, in turn, are held in the fabric of our creation."

PAGE 5

Jacob
Throw
Joan Berner & Linda Geiger, New York

Leah, a Jacob ewe from Linda Geiger's flock, grew this wool. Linda spun the yarn. Joan Berner wove the throw, after they overdyed some skeins with blue acid dyes.

PAGE 9

Villsau (Old Norwegian)
Baby Socks
Trygve Fjarli & Ruth Volden, Norway

Villsau, also known as Old Norwegian breed, has been connected to

the remains of sheep approximately 3,000 years old. Villsau sheep survive today because people on the islands of the western coast of Norway value them. These sheep behave unusually in response to threats and successfully graze where large predators, like bears and wolves, are active. Trygve Fjarli spun the wool for these stockings on a traditional Norwegian spinning wheel, and Ruth Volden knitted them.

PAGE 10

Cotswold
Bad Hair Day
Anne Williams, Connecticut

Anne Williams has raised longwool sheep in a New York City suburb for thirty-six years. Her hat was inspired by her love for Cotswolds, who have "superb temperaments and unsurpassed long, soft, lustrous curls which take natural dyes beautifully." Anne spins on a wheel her twice-great grandmother brought from Holland in 1820. She used textured singles for the knitted base of the hat, and solidly secured between fifty and sixty locks in the structure. She sells lots of these natural-colored hats to men, women, and teens.

PAGE 12

California Variegated Mutant
Kerry Blue Shawl
Diane Bentley-Baker, Texas

For this shawl, Diane Bentley-Baker spun natural-gray wool grown by Hertz #1 from Palanka Farms, Waxahachie, Texas. She says it was "a joy to make because of the wonderful CVM wool, which fortunately is becoming a favorite in Texas." Wool quality increases as spinners provide shepherds with feedback, because husbandry practices influence the fibers' length, strength, and cleanliness.

California Variegated Mutant
Flora's Socks
Robin Lynde, California

This is Robin Lynde's first completed pair of socks, made with Navajo-plied yarn from her CVM ewe, Flora.

California Variegated Mutant
Mogollon Shawl
Jacquie Kelly, Arizona

Jacquie processed her CVM fleece on Viking combs, then spun a two-ply yarn. She did not control color shadings before knitting, but she placed darker skeins at the beginning and end of the shawl. Her shawl's shaping, knitting, and border follow Russia's Orenburg lace tradition. She charted the center of the shawl after a fragment of openwork weaving found at Mule Creek Cave in New Mexico, shown in Kate Peck Kent's *Prehistoric Textiles of the American Southwest*. The shawl is named Mogollon (*MOW-ghee-yon*) for its Southwestern heritage.

PAGE 16

Navajo Churro
Vest
D. Phillip Sponenberg, Virginia

Phil Sponenberg works with ALBC and is interested in color genetics. He writes, "A few years back, ALBC gave me a twenty-year service award, one of the neatest honors I've had. Hearing about this, Connie Taylor [Cerro Mojino Woolworks, New Mexico] sent samples of her moorit Navajo Churro sheep. I spun them up and knitted myself an 'award vest,' which reminds

me of the great people (generous, too) involved in this conservation work."

Navajo Churro
Shawl
Kathrin Olson-Rutz, Montana

Kathrin Olson-Rutz and her husband raise sheep at Paintbrush Navajo-Churro. Her shawl—home grown, hand shorn, handspun, and hand knitted—was inspired by Robert Powell's triangular shawls in *Spin-Off*, Winter 1996.

PAGE 20

Shetland
Shawl
Beth Caddell, Indiana

Beth calls this a "half-shawl," a triangle constructed like a traditional square Shetland lace shawl. She hand-carded a lamb's fleece to preserve the color variations and spun a two-ply yarn. The patterns for the shawl's body came from Barbara Walker's books, and its edging from a shawl by Hazel Carter.

PAGE 22

Walachenschaf
Bath Scrubber
Baerbel Epprecht, Germany

Walachenschaf date to the thirteenth century, but only about two hundred existed by 1998. Frau Kinzelmann, who supplied the fleece, has most of her wool spun and woven into rugs and bench covers. With a wide-toothed comb, Baerbel Epprecht separated the outer coat from the under coat—and discovered three fiber types: the long, protective outer coat; the short, finer undercoat; and a downy inner coat. Baerbel and her husband decided yarn spun from the middle coat reminded them of knitted sisal back scrubbers, so she crocheted a deluxe bath accessory from tightly twisted singles.

PAGE 23

Cotswold
The Homeplace 1850 Collection
Scarf, Hat, & Wrist Warmers
Jackie Cravens, Cindy Earls, &
Amanda Nikkel, Kentucky & Tennessee

These historical garments were produced at The Homeplace 1850, a living history museum representing a family farm in the mid-nineteenth century. Located in the Land Between The Lakes, Tennessee, The Homeplace 1850 maintains minor-breed livestock, including Cotswold sheep. After selecting the finest fleece from the spring shearing, the staff women used historic methods of carding, spinning, and dyeing (with logwood and marigolds) and then knitted a woman's scarf, a pair of children's *muf-fatees* (fingerless mittens worn over gloves during sleigh rides), and a woman's *cephaline* (winter cap).

PAGE 24

Pommersches Landschaf
Sweater
Patricia Stein, Germany

Pommersches Landschaf originated along the Baltic Sea and almost vanished by 1982. Lambs of this breed start out black, then fade to a full range of grays and gray-browns. The sheep are double coated, so Patricia Stein separated out the fine undercoat to drum-card for her soft sweater.

Cotswold
Socks
Noreen Muellerweiss, Michigan

Noreen Muellerweiss keeps both black and white Cotswolds. She says these socks, knitted from heavy singles yarn, support Cotswold's reputation as "the poor man's mohair."

Romeldale
Christening Shawl
Phyllis Karsten, California

This Romeldale wool came from Phyllis Karsten's flock. The ewe's first shearing yielded 14 pounds (6.3 kg) of raw fiber. Phyllis washed it to preserve the lock structure, flicked open the ends, and drum-carded the wool. She spun singles and wove three related fabrics on a huck threading from Helene Bress' *The Weaving Book*. One fabric became this shawl; one became a beloved, well-worn shirt; the third awaits its purpose.

Brillenschaf
Viking Sweater
Alexandra Weikert, Germany

These are called "spectacles sheep" because they have black patches on their faces and ears that make them look like they're wearing glasses. A friend of Alexandra Weikert's provided the wool, which was washed and carded in Bavaria and gilled in England. Alexandra found her pattern choice to be the hardest part of this endeavor. She chose a design by Elsebeth Lavold.

Jacob
Norwegian-style Mittens
Alice Gillespie, Pennsylvania

These mittens are made of two-ply Jacob. The palm and cuff patterns came from Elizabeth Zimmermann's *Knitting Around*. Alice adapted the pattern on the backs of the hands from a sweater by Jean Frost in *Knitter's*, Fall 1993.

Jacob
Scarf of Many Colors
Suzanne Jones, Missouri

Suzanne Jones chose Jacob for its historical significance and colors. Using wool from a ewe in her flock named Rebecca, she spun a Navajo-plied yarn. She developed her weaving structure with the name draft technique, which changes words to a threading sequence. Suzanne's draft encodes "ALBC; Please help Spin-Off save a sheep; spin a yarn from an endangered breed; RBST." She says, "Wool is a renewable resource, so I can spin Rebecca again next year!"

Cotswold
Lace Project
Debi Lee, Tennessee

Debi Lee was unable to finish her entry for the Save the Sheep project; she died in a traffic accident six weeks before the deadline. Her friends and family submitted her work in her name and in her memory. They say, "Debi had a particular knack for spinning fine yarns from coarse wools" and ending up with wonderful fabric. This was evident in her work in progress, where the yarn and the lace structure seem made for each other when lightly stretched to simulate the effect after blocking. Debi was an avid reader, and an article in her guild's newsletter suggests that donations be made in her name to a library. Perhaps libraries near the readers of this book would welcome books on spinning or rare-breed livestock.

Lincoln Longwool
Fan-stitch Half-circle Shawl
Pat Noah, Colorado

Pat Noah liked the shine and long staple of this Lincoln fleece, grown by Smokey under the care of Myrtle Dow, Black Pines Sheep, Eaton, Colorado. Her pattern comes from Martha Waterman's *Traditional Knitted Lace Shawls*.

Wensleydale
Bobble-cuffed Socks
Jeannine Bakriges, Vermont

Wensleydale sheep grow long, sturdy, shiny, and smooth wool—perfect for knitted socks that will last for years of comfortable wear. Jeannine Bakriges was given some white Wensleydale wool. She used brazilwood dust (genus *Caesalpinia*) to achieve this maroon shade, with alum and cream of tartar to assist the bonding of colorant and fiber. Both alum and cream of tartar can be found in the spice aisle of any grocery store.

Jeannine spent three years working with fibers as a historical interpreter at Black Creek Pioneer Village, in Toronto, Ontario (Canada). She lives with her husband, son, and cat in a Vermont loft.

Navajo Churro
Dibé b'iiná' (Sheep is Life)
Lena Benally, Arizona

Dibé b'iiná' means "sheep is life" in Navajo, and the phrase reflects the profound relationship between traditional Navajo life and Navajo Churro sheep, who are well adapted to the challenging landscape of the American Southwest.

Lena Benally tends about fifty Navajo Churro sheep on a mesa in Arizona. She used her traditional spindle to spin her yarn. She made the warp from Cotswold wool (warp yarns provide the foundation for the fabric, but don't contribute to the pattern). The weft yarns, which make the visible pattern, demonstrate the colors of Navajo Churro wool. The Navajo weaving style called Two Grey Hills refers to textiles constructed of handspun yarn and natural-colored fibers, most often grown by Navajo Churro sheep.

Shetland
Tiger Eye Shawl
Cynthia Heeren
Oregon

Shetland
Knitted Lace Scarf
Jane Burton
Missouri

PAGE 34

Tunis
One fleece = one sheep = Tunis!
Johanna Bolton, Florida

Tunis sheep, now fully American, first arrived in 1799 as a gift from the ruler of Tunisia. This woven sheep incorporates about three-quarters of a Tunis fleece—the body is even stuffed with wool. The face color comes from black walnuts.

Tunis sheep are long-lived, hardy, disease-resistant, and able to survive on marginal land. They're calm sheep and produce a lot of milk (some are used in sheep dairies, especially those which make feta cheese). Johanna Bolton spun part of the yarn for her sheep on a wheel and part on a hand spindle, which she used while wandering around craft shows and powwows. She wove the fabric on a simple loom. Johanna originally learned to spin when she got tired of sweeping up dog hair and decided to do something productive with it.

Cotswold
Knitted and Felted Hat
Margaret Boos, California

Margaret Boos has been raising sheep and spinning for about twenty years. Her sheep wear coats to keep their wool cleaner. Cotswold is Margaret's favorite wool.

"If you're going to make something you want to last, why not start with good-quality materials?" Margaret backs up her words by raising her own sheep. Her husband shears, then Margaret makes hats, purses, scarves, and other items. She likes to spin heavy, textured yarns, for which Cotswold's weight and length are perfect. To make a hat like this, she knits the fabric large, then shrinks and felts it in a washing machine. While the fabric is wet, she individually shapes each hat on a mold.

PAGE 35

Cotswold & Navajo Churro
Cotswold Lock Jacket
Laurie Boyer, Illinois

Cotswolds produce *big* fleeces with *long* fibers. In one year, a sheep named Ears grew 19 pounds (8.6 kg) of wool, enough to make about six big sweaters. Laurie Boyer designed this knitted jacket to showcase Ears' beautiful locks.

Laurie combined wool from two endangered breeds in this jacket, which her mother-in-law is waiting to wear. Most of the fiber you see is Cotswold, but within the yarn Laurie designed to display the long Cotswold hides a bit of Navajo Churro as well, from a sheep named Ovaltine. The buttons, made from natural objects, are as varied in texture, color, and substance as the wools which went into the garment.

PAGE 36

Wensleydale
Scarf
Brenda Bryon, East Sussex,
United Kingdom

Five natural colors of long, shiny, silky Wensleydale appear in this knitted scarf, which weighs about 15 grams (a little over ½ ounce). You need a long, supple wool to spin this fine and make a fabric this airy!

Often the white and natural-colored

strains of a breed are kept separate, and this is the case with Wensleydales. The dominant genes produce white, so colored Wensleydales are even rarer than white ones. Wensleydales carry a resistance to scrapie, an illness which has severely affected many sheep breeds. Very fine for a long wool, Wensleydale fiber can be damaged by commercial treatment. It's ideally suited for careful hand processing, and this finished scarf is far sturdier than it looks.

PAGE 37

California Variegated Mutant
"Coming Home" Shawl
Kaye Collins, Colorado

Before making this knitted shawl, Kaye Collins spent years working with alpaca, a fiber very different from wool. When she turned to this project, she says it "felt like coming home" to wool.

Romeldales and CVMs are closely related producers of fine wool: Romeldales in white, CVMs in browns, grays, blacks, and spotted variations. Kaye's design varies a concept developed by Jackie Erickson-Schweitzer (see her Cotswold blanket, page 39), which in turn draws on traditional lace shawls from the Shetland Islands. The lace-pattern stitch that travels across the years from the Shetlands to Jackie to Kay is "Feather and Fan." Kaye blended 80 percent CVM with 20 percent silk to give her shawl the benefits of both fibers' qualities.

Navajo Churro
Churro Hat
Laurie Boyer, Illinois

Navajo Churros produce relatively small fleeces—enough for one or two sweaters, or a handful of hats. Wool from young animals is softer than wool from mature ones, and Laurie Boyer used a yearling fleece for her knitted hat.

Navajo Churro wool grows in two distinct layers, one finer, softer, and shorter than the other. Laurie separated the layers in this fleece, using the coarser fiber to make loops in one of her yarns while the finer fiber holds the yarn together. Laurie calls her hat "fanciful, but functional," and hopes "its humor touches you, as the joy of spinning and knitting it has touched me."

PAGE 38

Shetland
Flock
Teresa Gardner, Missouri

The tesselated design of this sweater incorporates many natural colors of Shetland wool. All except the white came from Teresa Gardner's small flock. She spun wool from nine sheep into eleven yarns.

Teresa says, "The disappearance of these wonderful animals saddens me greatly. From the moment I read about the plans for the exhibit, I was distracted. Two months of struggling and talks with my daughter, Rachelle, led me to tesselation: forms that fit together like a puzzle. The loss of any one form leaves a hole, an incompleteness. From the creation of the design to the shearing of our sheep, to the spinning and knitting, a bit of my soul is in this sweater."

Navajo Churro
Macramé Change Purse
Mary Ellen ("Melon") Corsini and
Diane Ballerino-Regan, North Carolina

Navajo Churro fleece often contains two distinct types of fiber. Diane Ballerino-Regan spun the coarse guard hairs from three fleeces for Melon

Skudde

Hat & Scarf

Beka Rewerts
Germany

Corsini, who wanted firm, fine yarn to use in macramé, a knotting technique.

Melon is a self-taught macramé artist and Diane (a proficient handspinner) is her physician. Conversation during a routine checkup resulted in the collaboration which produced two pieces, both in this show. Diane spun gray yarn (four *very* thin strands, combined in the finished yarn) and dyed it with cochineal, a natural red. A diamond pattern of double half-hitches forms the body of this change purse.

During the 1970s, macramé was used to make lots of clunky plant hangers. Melon here restores the technique to grace, dignity, and contemporary utility.

Navajo Churro
Round Mat
Mary Ellen ("Melon") Corsini and
Diane Ballerino-Regan, North Carolina

This small mat by spinner Diane

Ballerino-Regan and macramé artist Melon Corsini combines yarns from three sheep tended by Jean and Tracy Eichheim in Colorado: Nina (light gray), #18 (black), and Portia (gray, natural-dyed with red). The sheep wore coats to keep their growing wool clean.

Although knotted, this piece appears to have been coiled (a technique used for baskets). Melon started in the middle with a core of four yarns and half-hitched around, adding threads as the piece grew. By the last row, she was individually knotting more than three hundred pieces of yarn over the core. She wove the end of each piece invisibly into the back of the mat.

PAGE 39

Cotswold
Lace Blanket
Jackie Erickson-Schweitzer, Louisiana

Jackie Erickson-Schweitzer calls this "moose lace," because it's knitted at a large scale. A solid blanket of Cotswold, dense and supple, would be very heavy. The lacey holes lighten this fabric to about two pounds (900 grams).

While Cotswolds come in colors, this natural golden gray is extremely unusual. Because of the color, Jackie worked hard to remove pulverized seeds and plant debris from the wool and to prepare it for spinning into a yarn which incorporated a lot of air, for softness and lighter weight. She says, "At several times throughout the cleaning and preparation, I thought about just pitching the rest of the wool into the garden." Fortunately, when she got through the preliminary ordeal the spinning went well. The knitting, too, proceeded smoothly, although Jackie says "it wasn't very portable."

PAGE 40

Navajo Churro, Spelsau, Karakul, & Gotland
Window to the Past . . .
View of the Future?
Priscilla Gibson-Roberts, Colorado

To spin her fine yarns, Priscilla Gibson-Roberts used wool from four "primitive" breeds and a small han spindle, like the one shown. She knitted the authentic designs on tiny, specially made needles. Socks traditionally have been made from these wools.

From left to right, the socks (and wools) are Afghan (Spelsau), Norwegian (Gotland), Turkish (Navajo Churro lamb's wool), Norwegian (Spelsau), and Iranian (Navajo Churro). The skeins are Karakul, overdyed, and there's Navajo Churro on the spindle. Priscilla says, "I don't know whether I have made a nostalgic window to the past, or a rather bleak view of the future. Nostalgia isn't sufficient to save the sheep, and without these fibers there is little hope of mantaining textile traditions perfected through eons."

PAGE 41

Wensleydale
Scarf
Suzi Gough, APO/United Kingdom

Here's a fabric which overlays a lattice of handspun wool from an endangered breed, Wensleydale, on a background of commercially spun fine Merino wool. Neither breed could substitute for the other.

Suzi Gough inherited her love of weaving from her grandmother, Ilse Etta Uhlmann. Suzi is new to spinning—this is the first time she has used her handspun yarn in a project. Many experienced fiber artists discover that spinning opens doors to creativity they hadn't known existed. People with no fiber background who learn from a good spinning teacher find out that the basics are easy, while there are always new horizons to explore.

Shetland
Swedish-inspired Sweater
Greater Birmingham Fiber Guild, Alabama

One pleasure of spinning is that you can work solo or collaborate. To make this sweater-jacket, members of the Greater Birmingham Fiber Guild combined their skills in preparation, spinning, knitting, weaving, and sewing.

Eight members saw the project through from raw fleece to finished garment: Pia Cusick, Karen Ford, Mary Geier, Barbara Gower, Mary Kaiser, Terry Martin, Debbie Scott, and Mary Spanos. Additional people helped sort, wash, and card (fluff) the raw wool from two fleeces (light and dark), which differed dramatically in fineness, length, and ease of working. Processing began in June and ended in November. The body was woven and the sleeves were knitted. When the sweater returns from its tour it will belong to one member (a surprise gift from the others).

PAGE 42

Navajo Churro
Ojas del Otoño
Rita Padilla Haufmann, New Mexico

Navajo Churro wool provides the foundation for three weaving traditions in the American Southwest: the Rio Grande, Hopi, and Navajo. Rita Padilla Haufmann's work, of handspun, natural-colored and natural-dyed yarn, is based in the Rio Grande style.

This tapestry depends on a five-band pattern, with small stripes within each larger panel. Natural colors form the background, against which lie corals dyed with a plant called madder (*Rubia tinctorum*). Rita says, "I incorporated tapestry sections in angular shapes of diamonds in alternating colors to give the impression of movement, reminiscent of leaves falling in autumn, or *Ojas del Otoño.*" Two of Rita's many-times-great grandmothers were listed on the 1823 census as stocking knitters, so she weaves a small stocking as a signature.

Shetland
Ragg Socks
Catherine Lampman, Tennessee

Throughout history, the wools grown by local—now endangered—sheep have been used to make pragmatic textiles which aren't in museums because they were worn until they could be worn no more.

Catherine Lampman designed these socks for her husband. She wanted them to be warm, light, and longwearing. Tennessee winters can be cold and wet, like those in the Shetland Islands. Knitted at 8 ½ stitches to the inch (2.5 cm), the fabric is finer than that in many commercial socks. Ragg yarn is made by spinning light and dark strands together. You can find ragg socks in a lot of catalogs today. Here's the real thing: a work of everyday art.

PAGE 43

Pitt Island Merino
A Shawl for Great-Grandmother
Betty Kelly, New Zealand

Merino sheep provide most of the fine wool used commercially and are not rare at all. Pitt Island Merinos, a separate breed native to a set of islands over 500 miles east of mainland New Zealand, are another matter entirely.

Betty Kelly describes these remote islands, located just west of the international date line, as "a mystically desolate place whose meagerness makes clear the difficulty of sustaining life on earth." Betty says, "I initially declined the offer of a Pitt Island fleece. The fibers look short, but stretch to almost double and spin an amazingly elastic thread—not easy to deal with. But when my great-grandparents arrived in New Zealand by sailing ship in the mid-1850s, these sheep were already here. I decided to make a shawl in memory of my great-grandmother."

Manx Loghtan
Scarf and Cap
Heather Maxey, British Columbia, Canada

Vikings introduced Manx Loghtan sheep to the Isle of Man when they used the island as a supply site for further conquests. *Manx* means "from the Isle of Man" and *Loghtan* means "mouse-colored," a reference to the soft, brown wool.

The Isle of Man is located in the Irish Sea midway between England, Scotland, Ireland, and Wales. It isn't part of the United Kingdom, and never has been, although the United Kingdom provides passports, defense, and representation overseas. There are no Manx sheep in North America. Their wool is always brown, spins easily, is lofty (warm and lightweight), and feels exceptionally soft. Heather Maxey learned to knit from her grandmother about sixty-seven years ago. The pattern for her scarf, called a *tucker,* was popular in the 1930s.

PAGE 44

Shetland
Scarf
Joanne Littler, Vermont

Simple elegance comes from the best

materials crafted with care. Joanne Littler chose Shetland wool for her scarf because of its inherent lightweight softness. She wove the fabric on a counterbalanced loom, a sturdy type suited to making household fabrics.

Not so long ago, families and itinerant handweavers made all the fabrics required for daily life, as well as for more extraordinary uses: sheets, pillowcases, towels, clothing, ships' sails, the silken envelopes of hot air balloons. Part of what they got in exchange for their labor—and handcrafting textiles takes time—was the pleasure of creating and using fabrics perfectly suited their end purposes. In this twill-woven scarf, Joanne honors the multitude of skills required to accomplish such a goal. And she says, "A great deal of the credit belongs to Linda Doane, for her flock's wonderful wool."

California Variegated Mutant
Socks
Jan Viren, Minnesota

Where do you find rare wools? Many spinners first encounter fleeces from endangered breeds at regional wool festivals. Jan Viren acquired her fiber at the Taos Wool Festival, which takes place in New Mexico every fall.

Simple pleasures: pure wool, well spun and knitted. A pair of socks for hard-working feet. Wool from CVMs is soft enough to feel good, yet well-twisted in the spinning it becomes durable as well. Jan planned to make a man's pair of socks, but the amount of wool she had dictated the finished dimensions as well as the light-colored toes. If you want boring, predictable socks, there are plenty available through standard outlets. These have character. The sheep provided the colors.

Shetland
Sunset Kimono
Sara Lamb, California

Sara Lamb spun her two-ply yarn of 80 percent Shetland wool and 20 percent silk, and carefully dyed the yarns with five synthetic colors before weaving. She wove two fabrics: a body fabric and a band fabric.

Sara says, "The colors remind me of a sunset I saw from a plane in 1975. At that altitude, the sun setting under a bank of clouds created deep, rich colors. I tried to reproduce the sunset with commercial yarns, with poor results. Twenty-four years later, dyeing the yarns allows me to reproduce the range of colors. Painting warps blends adjacent colors, creating an effect similar to colors in nature, where colors shift by fading from one to another. I did not set out to paint that memory, but as I dyed the yarns the sunset returned."

Rhoenschaf
At shepherds' fair in Thuringia. Photo courtesy of William Epprecht.

Shetland
Fair Isle Coat
Shetland Guild of Spinners, Weavers, and Dyers, Shetland Islands, Scotland

The Shetland Islands lie north of mainland Scotland, in the North Sea. Small and very hardy, Shetland sheep grow wool in a wider array of natural colors than any other breed of sheep. Each color has a traditional Gaelic name.

Shetland Islanders—the people—have used this wool to develop distinct and strong knitting traditions. Shetland lace shawls, represented elsewhere in this exhibit, exemplify one type of knitting. Another tradition is Fair Isle design (named for one island in the group). In Fair Isle knitting, simple color patterns are combined to build complex designs. The Shetland Guild of Spinners, Weavers, and Dyers made this patchwork sampler coat to show the colors grown by the islands' native sheep and how Fair Isle patterns work.

Shetland
Lace Scarf
Anne Silk, Prince Edward Island, Canada

In addition to coming in wonderful natural colors, Shetland wool is soft enough to make sweaters and shawls, and sturdy enough to wear well. This lace scarf draws inspiration from the Shetland lace-shawl knitting tradition. The color of the wool is called *moorit*.

Anne Silk spun her yarn from a first-shearing fleece of lamb's wool, the finest and softest wool a sheep produces in its lifetime. From that fleece, she chose the finest and softest sections. Her finished shawl measures 42 by 27 inches (107 by 69 cm) and weighs ⅞ ounce (25 g). The patterns she used come from three different sources. She spent 390 hours flicking the locks open, rolling them, spinning, washing, knitting, blocking, and finishing her scarf.

Cotswold
Vest
Robin Metzger, Oregon

Robin Metzger's small flock of Cotswolds contains nine white and eight black sheep. All the natural grays in this knitted vest came from a six-month lamb's fleece grown by a sheep named Margarete.

Cotswold is sometimes called "poor man's mohair" because of the length and shine of the fibers. Margarete's fleece contains many shades of gray, which Robin separated into four distinct colors before she spun three strands of each color, which she plied together. By using these yarns in sequence, she made a vest whose coloration resembles that of Margarete's shorn coat (Margarete, busy growing a new fleece, turned a year old as the exhibit was installed for the first time).

California Variegated Mutant
Byzantine Vest
Sarah Swett, Idaho

"Despite its unconventional name," says Sarah Swett, "CVM is a delicious fleece, open and bouncy. The natural colors shine, but the wool also dyes beautifully." Her knitted vest uses both color patterns and textured stitches.

Sarah likes to tell stories with wool. She calls her vest "Byzantine" because it brings to mind the colors and activities of an Eastern marketplace. Her colors come from natural sources—indigo for blues (*Indigofera* spp.), madder for reds (*Rubia tinctorum*), and kamala for brilliant yellows (*Mallotus philippinensis*).

Karakul
Red Karakul Rug
Barbara Kent Stafford, California

Karakul sheep originate in the

Middle East. They produce fiber you can walk on for years before it shows wear. Natural colors range from black to gray, from creamy white to beige and caramel-red. The reds are rarest.

Barbara Kent Stafford weaves rugs, and has used Karakul wool for more than fifteen years because it is so "bold and sturdy." For this project, she looked specifically for the elusive reds and found them in lamb fleeces, "all long and silken with tight little ringlets at the ends." Many of the wools featured in this show are fine and soft, or are long, shiny, and supple. Karakul has body. Karakul will last. This rug—after hard use—could look this good when all of us are gone.

Jacob
Colleen's Coat
Mary Underwood and Rebecca Lambers, Michigan

Jacob sheep take their name from the Biblical story of Jacob. The ancient breed has obscure origins, but a most distinctive appearance: all Jacobs have spots, and both rams and ewes carry fine, great horns.

Mary Underwood spun the yarn and wove the fabric for this jacket, which Rebecca Lambers designed and sewed. The piece is named for the sheep who grew most of the wool, Colleen (helped by her sister, Isabel). Mary separated Colleen's black wool (which grows from black skin) from her white (from white or pink skin). Where the fiber colors intermingled, she set sections aside to make gray. Although Mary is an accomplished seamstress, she decided to collaborate with Rebecca on this jacket. She says, "I have loved the experience. It's more fun that I could have imagined."

Navajo Churro
Turtledove in Red
Ellen Sullivan, California

Ellen Sullivan recently decided that she would no longer weave her Southwestern-style rugs with commercial yarns. Having obtained two Navajo Churro ewes, she began to spin their wool.

She says, "This rug is made predominantly from the wool of a ewe named Turtledove. The strong, clear, geometric design represents her headstrong character. She is meek most of the time, but under that lustrous coat-of-armor is a warrior ewe!" Navajo Churros are noted for their ability to thrive in the rugged landscape of New Mexico and Arizona, where both water and vegetation are scarce. Attempts to "improve" the sheep of the region—so that individual animals produce more wool and meat—have been hard on the land, the sheep, and the people who depend on both.

CVM/Romeldale
Cyclone Vest
Diane Ballerino-Regan, North Carolina

Diane Ballerino-Regan knitted this vest from white Romeldale and two shades of CVM to commemorate the six hurricanes and one tropical storm she experienced in four years. She spun two-ply and four-ply cable yarns. She says, "The darkest spirals represent the worst hurricanes, Floyd and Fran. The lighter gray represents Bonnie and Bertha, which were not as severe. The white spirals represent two near misses, Dennis and Irene, as well as tropical storm Josephine."

Rhoenschaf
Inkle-band Hanging
Baerbel Epprecht
Germany

Cotswold
Seamus' Vest
Tri-Community Adult Education
Weaving and Spinning Class,
Covina, California

All participants in this effort were adult education students except Seamus, the sheep who provided the silver Cotswold wool. Barbara Osborne coordinated the venture. Spinners included Eileen Ditsler, Barbara Osborne, Gwena Tessier, and Marie Villareal. Marie knitted the vest.

Cotswold
Shawl
Susan Anne Metz, Missouri

Susan Anne Metz space-dyed three lots of wool with Kool-Aid and blended them on a drum carder before knitting her shawl.

Dorset Horn
Socks
Frances Irving, Manitoba, Canada

The wool came from a ewe in Frances Irving's flock. She sheared, washed, carded, dyed, and knitted it. The color comes from onion skins.

Dorset Horn
Socks
Martha Williams, Iowa

Martha wanted to show how nicely Dorset Horn (the white wool) works for socks. The patterns, traditional to the Shetland Islands, are worked in Shetland. All wools came from Judy Colvin, Bitterroot Ranch, Montana.

Gulf Coast Native
Aran-patterned Vest
Patricia Piehota, Oklahoma

Patricia Piehota raises Gulf Coast Native sheep. Her vest pattern came from Alice Starmore's work. You can't see in the photo how stunningly lightweight and lofty this fabric is. It probably provides more warmth per bouncy ounce than most fabrics we've seen.

Gulf Coast Native
Helen's Slipper Socks
Maureen Burnett, Mississippi

Maureen Burnett chose Gulf Coast Native wool because it's native to Mississippi. Maureen obtained ready-to-spin roving and made slipper socks for her eldest daughter, using natural cream for the cuff and toe. The pink and rust colors came from Kool-Aid.

Hog Island
Slipper Socks
Gail Johnson, Minnesota

Gail Johnson knitted these slipper socks for her husband, Bob, using Hog Island fleece because he grew up in Virginia and before they met he raised hogs for a while. She says he loves hand made socks, because his feet are hard to fit commercially. Gail's pattern, the classic sock from Nancy Bush's *Folk Socks,* has a half-handkerchief heel.

Hog Island
Sunston Shawl
Sara Gene Posnett, Pennsylvania

Sara Gene Posnett says, "Hog Island sheep are raised for their historical and educational value at Gunston Hall Plantation in northern Virginia, at Mount Vernon, and across the Potomac River at National Colonial Farm, in Accokeek, Maryland." The wool was donated by Gunston Hall Plantation. She spun this yarn during school programs at Mount Vernon, and wove the shawl on her late father's counterbalance loom, made in 1956 by Milton Gavetti of Media, Pennsylvania.

Jacob
Afghan
Manitoba Handspinners,
Manitoba, Canada

Eight people—Heather Adamson, Brigitte de March, Fran Irving, Carol James, Francine Ruiter, Jo-Anne Tabachek, Mieke von Massow, and Edna Wooler—made this afghan. One person washed, carded, sorted, and weighed the fleece, and composed packets containing six shades. Six members spun and then knitted or wove two squares each. The eighth member assembled the

squares and crocheted the borders. They "were amazed at how different the squares looked, considering that each person started with the same materials."

Karakul
Barn Angel
Marjorie Mills, Michigan

Marjorie Mills made the head for this "flying sheep doll" from Fimo in a class, then didn't have a clue what to do with it—until evening brought dreams of an angel to "watch over our endangered breeds forever." The corespun novelty yarn and felted wings are Karakul; the cuffs, neckline, and waistband of the sheep's sweater are Tunis; the stuffing is Finn wool.

Karakul
Bag
Peggy Siders, Indiana

Peggy Siders combined three natural-colored Karakul fleeces in this bag, which she has used as a purse for many years. It looks brand new—a testament to Karakul's durability.

Leicester Longwool
Raspberries & Cream Wrap
Rae Jean Rimmer, Virginia

Here's shine, drape, and elegance. The acid-dyed colors owe their clarity to the Leicester Longwool fiber.

Lincoln Longwool
Wild Asters
Dobree Adams, Kentucky

When Dobree Adams began raising Lincolns in 1986, they were on ALBC's conservation list. The breed is still listed as endangered by the RBST. Changes in status reflect the successes of individual people working on behalf of specific breeds. Dobree spins her Lincolns' wool into smooth and textured yarns, then hand-paints the skeins. She says, "My work is focused on protecting the environment. The sheep not only provide the raw material for my weaving but also a direct line of communication between my woven work and the earth."

PAGE 61

Manx Loghtan
Vest
Edna Smith, Alberta, Canada

The body of this vest is a woven twill; its lapels are knitted in moss-stitch, with silk embroidery. Edna Smith was not completely satisfied, because the fiber was short and felted a bit when washed. The jurors were impressed with the soft hand, craftsmanship, and delicate balances in textures, colors, and surfaces.

PAGE 62

Navajo Churro
Scarf #3
Connie Taylor, New Mexico

Connie Taylor worked with Navajo Churro wool from her own flock, as well as from the flocks of Ingrid Painter and Barb Barraclough. She calls her red scarf "Cha-Cha Churro." It's woven from two-ply yarn in a dornik twill.

PAGE 63

North Ronaldsay
Socks
Deborah Pulliam, Maine

Deborah Pulliam "was fascinated by the North Ronaldsay sheep (also known as Orkney) because they live on a remote island on the beach, eating seaweed." After lots of effort, she obtained white and gray fleeces, planning to make patterned socks. As she worked with the gray, she decided to experiment with plain socks. We didn't want to send them back, but Deborah knows where to find us, so we did.

North Ronaldsay
Sock
Danette Pratt, Ohio

Danette Pratt based her sock design on "Socks for Troll Children," in *Socks, Socks, Socks: 70 Winning Patterns from the Knitter's Magazine Contest,* edited by Elaine Rowley. Danette modified the pattern to fit an adult troll and intends to make a second sock. She has a longstanding interest in heritage livestock breeds. Her interest in North Ronaldsays began when she read *Rare Breeds* (Dowling, Alderson, and Caras).

PAGE 64

Ryeland
Miniature Stocking
Sammie Oaks, New Mexico

Sammie Oaks' sister-in-law in England sent Ryeland wool from her farm in a vacuum-packed container, prepared by the local butcher (who didn't ask why). Sammie used Mary Spanos' miniature stocking pattern from *Socks,* a *Spin-Off* publication edited by Rita Buchanan and Deborah Robson.

Ryeland
Mittens
Martha Williams, Iowa

Ryelands date to the twelfth century. Martha Williams wanted to show how useful their wool is for knitting. Her pattern came from *Homespun, Handknit,* edited by Linda Ligon, although she used Robin Hansen's method of two-end knitting.

PAGE 65

Santa Cruz Island
Wedding-ring Lace Shawl
Nancy Van Tassel, California

Nancy Van Tassel knitted her traditional shawl (it goes through a ring) from wool grown by Elsa, shown on pages 14–15. Nancy had an adventure locating wool from an endangered breed—and found it ten minutes from home. She says the wool is "elastic and tends to slub. I used a short draw, light tension, and lots of twist." Nancy had been "too timid" to try an idea she had for a shawl. Elsa's yarn got her going.

PAGE 66

Shetland
Socks
Vicki Ball, Vermont

Vicki Ball made two-ply gray Shetland yarn from a five-month fleece which the shearer thought was too short to spin (most fleeces are twelve-months' growth). Vicki decided it was too precious not to. The sheep, Bess, had been extremely shy until one day Bess decided she was Vicki's sheep—and "has never looked back."

Shetland
Shepherd's Spiral
Judi Lehrhaupt, Pennsylvania

Judi Lerhaupt says, "This cap was spun from the fleeces of three of my own sheep: Hershey (*moorit* in color), Othello (black), and Rosalind (grayish brown). I spun Hershey's yarn as a rank beginner, Othello's when I had a bit more practice, and Rosalind's more recently. The directions for the cap came from my mother's collection. When my sons were young, Mom knitted each of them a cap like this one. It is my delight to dedicate this project to the memory of my mother, Ruth Raff, an amazing artist, musician, and grand-mother."

Shetland
My Shetland Flock Vest
Joan Contraman, Montana

Joan Contraman's reversible vest commemorates her flock. For the hand-woven color-and-weave fabric, she combined black yarn from her ram, Damion, with a variegated yarn composed of Taffy's fawn wool, Balfour's white wool, and 10 percent silk, all dyed with blue, turquoise, and orchid. The other side is lightweight commercial wool fabric dyed in the same colors, with freehand portraits of the flock drawn with a fabric marking pen.

PAGE 67

Soay
Miniature Moss-stitch Helmet
Tan Summers, Utah

Tan Summers found Soay wool hard to locate—most Soays are in the United Kingdom, not Utah. She found some at a Scottish rare-breed park. The average fiber length was 1–2 inches (2.5–5 cm), "about like dryer lint" to spin. Her pattern came from Debbie Bliss' work.

Soay
Saint Kilda Scarf
Barbara Ballas, Oregon

Soay sheep come from the Saint Kilda Islands, west of the Outer Hebrides, Scotland, named a World Heritage Site. Humans lived on these islands from the Stone Age through the early 1930s. Barbara Ballas says, "This scarf is a small example of what the people of Saint Kilda may have made. Each year they paid their rent with hundreds of handknitted items and thousands of yards of woven tweed."

PAGE 68

Southdown
Tiny Sheep
Veronica de Olive-Lowe, New Zealand

Southdown sheep in North America have diverged from the breed's origins. Southdowns of the earlier sort are considered rare. Veronica de Olive-Lowe says that "of the fifty million or so sheep" in New Zealand "a bare handful are Southdown." Because Veronica found the short, dense fiber difficult to spin, she says, "I amused myself making the sheep. This is the way that sheep looked in my childhood in the 1930s and '40s." When we unpacked this perfect little sheep with seed-bead eyes, we marveled.

PAGE 69

Tunis
Mittens
Sharon Schulz, North Dakota

These Tunis mittens are both soft and sturdy. The angora around the cuffs keeps the wind out and warmth in.

PAGE 70

Wensleydale
Mittens
Marie Mercuri, Illinois

Marie Mercuri turned combed Wensleydale into a four-ply cable yarn for these mittens. Her pattern came from Robin Hansen's *Flying Geese and Partridge Feet.*

PAGE 74

Shetland
Tiger Eye Shawl
Cynthia Heeren, Oregon

Cynthia began with her attraction to this wool's deep natural *moorit* color. She chose a complex Tiger Eye pattern for the center, then kept the edging simple.

Shetland
Knitted Lace Scarf
Jane Burton, Missouri

Jane Burton achieved her goal of sending this lace scarf to the project "in support of rare sheep breeders." It's her first knitted lace project, and she says, "far from perfect," but she did a delightful job of matching fiber, yarn type, and application.

PAGE 75

Skudde
Hat & Scarf
Beka Rewerts, Germany

Skudde sheep originated in East Prussia and the Baltic states and are now under the care of the Alliance of Swiss Skudde Breeders. Most of these sheep are in Germany, with a few in Switzerland and Austria. Suited for pasturing in barren areas, they grow white, brown, black, and gray wool that combines a fine undercoat (delightful in this hat and scarf), short hairs, and long, coarse guard hairs.

PAGE 79

Rhoenschaf
Inkle-band Hanging
Baerbel Epprecht, Germany

The Rhoenschaf has existed since the sixteenth century, was common in the mid-nineteenth century, almost vanished by the 1960s, and is finding new work in landscape preservation. Baerbel Epprecht flick-combed and acid-dyed the wool, stained and full of second cuts and "barn residue." The animals are kept for breed conservation, and wool quality is not a priority. Baerbel says she wove to "represent the Rhoen, also called *land of open distances*," one of 320 areas worldwide designated as Biosphere Reserves. She says the fiber can be spun to a softer consistency for sturdy sweaters, socks, hats, or gloves.

THE CRAFT OF SPINNING

Basic ideas, tools, skills, and terms for handspinners

Starting with wool

Sheep's wool is the most popular fiber among handspinners because it is easy to spin and versatile. There are dozens of **breeds** of sheep, such as Lincoln, Romney, Corriedale, Suffolk, and Merino, and each breed produces a unique type of wool. By choosing from suitable breeds, spinners can use wool to make warm, comfortable, and stylish sweaters, scarves, mittens, hats, socks, afghans, rugs, and many other kinds of garments and accessories. One advantage to making your own yarn is that you can choose the qualities in the fiber that you want to emphasize in your finished project. Yes, the results are definitely worth it!

A single **fleece**—one sheep's annual growth of wool—usually weighs between 4 and 12 pounds. A good spinning fleece costs around $4 to $12 per pound. Shepherds who produce good wool pay extra attention to their animals throughout the year. Some put jackets, blankets, or **coats** on their sheep to keep hay out of the wool; those fleeces may be especially clean, although covering is not essential to the growing of good wool. Knowledge is. The best fleeces will have been **skirted** to remove any dirty, stained, or inferior wool; they will also contain only minimal amounts of hay, chaff, or burrs, which are hard to remove.

Wool fibers usually group together in clusters called **locks**. By gently pulling a few sample locks out of the fleece, you can determine the **staple length** (or average length) of the locks (usually between 3 and 8 inches), the **crimp** or waviness of the wool, and the **count** or thickness of the wool fibers (larger numbers indicate finer wool—80s is quite fine, and 40s is coarse). Coarse wool tends to have fewer crimps per inch, and may be scratchy or itchy-but will be very durable. Fine wool most often has a lot of crimps per inch, and feels soft and comfortable next to your skin, but would not wear well in a rug. These attributes can be measured precisely, but most spinners just assess them by eye and by feel.

In **raw** fleece, the fibers are coated with **grease** (lanolin and other natural body oils), condensed perspiration, and dust; all this is removed when the fleece is **washed** or **scoured**. Washing your own fiber is easy, although there are a few tricks to it. We suggest that you start with clean wool for your first efforts.[1]

Washing reveals any **luster** or shininess of the wool, and exposes its true

[1] But if what you've got is raw fleece, you don't have to rush to the store. When washing your own wool, remember: don't agitate, don't change water temperatures suddenly, and don't scrub. If you do all those things, you will produce felt, not clean, spinnable wool.

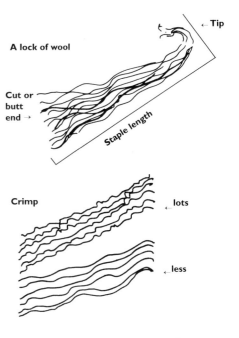

This information has been drawn from a variety of sources, including two introductory brochures on spinning which are available on request from Spin-Off for use by individuals or groups who do demonstrations or teaching. The entire content is included in these pages. One brochure covers basic terms and processes; the other describes how to start spinning with minimal equipment. Request copies from Spin-Off, Interweave Press, 201 E. 4th Street, Loveland, CO 80537, (970) 669-7672, www.interweave.com, spinoff@interweave.com.

Text by Rita Buchanan and Deborah Robson. Illustrations by Ann Sabin Swanson.

color, which may be pure white, off-white, yellowish, silver to charcoal gray, jet black, tan, or reddish brown. After washing, fleece can be **dyed in the wool,** or you can dye the spun yarn. Dyeing fleece is fun, because there are many ways to combine different colors into a single yarn with either very subtle or bold **variegation.**

Preparing the wool for spinning

Wool is easier to spin if it's **prepared** by separating the fibers into a loose, fluffy arrangement. You can buy a fleece and do the washing and preparation yourself, or pay a little more (usually $15 to $25 per pound) for wool that's been washed, dyed (if you choose), and processed.

Special tools have been designed for preparing wool and other fibers. A **flicker, flick carder,** or **pet comb** (average cost for the latter is under $10) is excellent for loosening individual locks and pulling out any short or weak fibers. **Flicking** works best for a fleece with distinct locks and a staple length of 4 inches or more. **Mini-combs, Viking combs,** and **English wool combs** (cost $50 to $150, and up) also work best for wool with locks that are at least 4 inches (10 cm) long. You can comb several locks at a time. **Combing** is a separating process—it removes any shorter fibers as it loosens and aligns the longer fibers. After combing, the long fibers are pulled into a smooth, continuous strand called a **top** (the short fibers are set aside for a different use or discarded); fibers can be pulled off with your fingers, or through a tool called a **diz** (a small disk with a hole in it). A few mills are set up to do combing, and sometimes you can buy commercially combed tops of wool or other fibers.

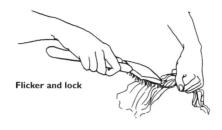

Flicker and lock

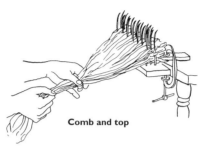

Comb and top

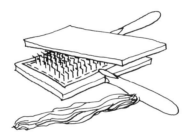

Hand cards and rolag

Drum carder and batt

Hand cards or **carders** (average cost $30 to $65) are good for preparing medium to short wool (staple length 4 inches/10 cm or less); **drum carders** (cost $150 to $500 or more) can handle short, medium, or long wool, depending on how they are set up. **Carding** is a blending process, good for evening out the variations in color, crimp, or length between different parts of a fleece; for blending different colors of dyed fleece; and for combining wool with mohair, angora, or other fibers. Wool can be lifted off a carder as a fluffy, pillow like, rectangular **batt.** Spinners sometimes roll batts into slender tubes called **rolags** or pull them lengthwise into long strands called **slivers** or **rovings.**[2] The carding process can easily be automated, and there are dozens of small mills around the United States that sell carded batts or rovings; some will custom-card wool that you supply.

Introduction to the hand spindle

Hand spindles provide a great introduction to spinning for the novice. At the same time, the most experienced spinners we know find this simple tool endlessly satisfying. A good spindle can be an excellent traveling companion, tucked in a briefcase, purse, backpack, or gym bag to help you fill odd moments at meetings or soccer games, in line at the department of motor vehicles, or watching television. If you

[2] When used with reference to commercially prepared fiber, the terms top, sliver, and roving are often applied interchangeably, although there are technical differences between these forms of prepared fiber.

haven't discovered the joy of using a fine hand spindle, you have a treat ahead of you.

Supply list

* 1 hand spindle, well balanced and not too heavy
* about ½ ounce (15 g) of prepared fiber, preferably medium-grade wool, in a color you like
* tiny piece of masking tape, with an arrow drawn on it
* a piece of wool starter yarn, about 24–30 inches (60–75 cm) long
* a little time
* a little patience
* a lot of fun

A *good spindle*

This is crucial. The wrong spindle will not let you discover the true pleasure of spinning, and the right one will do at least half the teaching. Some simple spindles work well, and some fancy ones don't. And vice versa.

There are many kinds of spindles, in all sizes, weights, and forms.

The basic elements include: **tip, hook, whorl, shaft.**

We're going to concentrate here on drop spindles. They have shafts that normally fall between 9 and 15 inches (23 and 38 cm) in length, and whorls between 2 and 3 inches (5 and 7.5 cm) across (although their whorls may be as small as 1½ inches [3.5 cm] or as large as 5 inches [13 cm]). Drop spindles twirl in mid-air as you spin, and are most often made of wood. Some have the whorl at the top of the shaft and some have it at the bottom. Either arrangement will do.

What makes a good spindle? You'll discover that in spinning there are no rules, but we can offer guidelines. (If you fall in love with a spindle that

There are two basic types of suspended (or drop) spindles: those used with the whorl at the top, and those used with the whorl at the bottom.

Regardless of type, a spindle needs to be well balanced ant to rotate smoothly and freely.

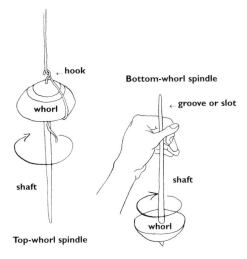

doesn't exactly fit our description, it might be perfect for you anyway.)

The weight depends on the type of yarn you want to spin—heavy yarn, heavy spindle. A drop spindle which weighs more than 4 ounces (115 g, or the substance of a medium-sized apple) is too heavy for general use. Hold off on the ½-ounce (15 g) spindle (with a whole-walnut's amount of gravity) until you have some experience. Look for a weight between 1½ and 2½ ounces (40 and 70 g, with the heft of an apricot or a plum).

Balance is essential. The location of the whorl on the shaft affects the spindle's balance, as does the shape of the whorl itself. Check a bottom-whorl spindle by resting its tip on a non-abrasive surface (like your leg) and giving it a twirl; let your fingers flick the shaft so it spins, and then make a circle of your fingers so the spindle can rotate freely but will remain upright. To check a top-whorl spindle, attach a short length of yarn to the hook at the top, give the shaft a quick roll between your fingers, and watch the spindle rotate. (The drawings above show this.)

Spin the spindle a few times. Then note your impressions. Does the spindle rotate freely (does it feel like it wants to spin) or does it wobble? Does it keep going for a while, or feel sluggish? Is the shaft easy to grasp and twirl? Do you like this spindle? If you have hesitations, keep looking; there are more spindles out there. Basically okay? Go for it!

Take the piece of tape with the arrow and put it on the whorl (those demo spindles above show how).

Some *puff*

Fiber, raw material, wool . . . you need something to spin. "Puff" is not an official name, but it does describe the quality you want your first fiber to have.

There are lots of reasons to prepare your own fiber, but there are also wonderful bags of ready-to-spin stuff out there which you can start on . . . or work with forever. With prepared fiber, you can spin now.

You want a medium-grade wool in batt or roving/sliver/top form (a batt is a pancake-like arrangement, and roving,

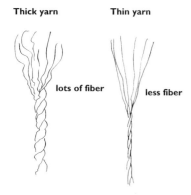

Thick yarn **Thin yarn**

lots of fiber   less fiber

The size of your yarn is determined by how much fiber is caught by the twist at any given point.

Top whorl **Bottom whorl**

Tie a starter yarn around the long portion of the spindle's shaft and take it through the hook or notch at the top of the spindle.

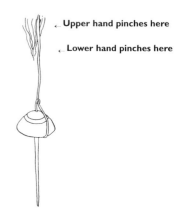

← **Upper hand pinches here**

← **Lower hand pinches here**

Your hands work together to draft the fiber and control the twist.

sliver, and top are rope-like). Let your senses guide your selection. The fiber should hang together well when you hold it gently, but it should have some air in it—like puff. (A slick, smooth preparation will be harder to work with until you're proficient.) Pick a color you like, either natural or dyed.

Separate a piece of your fiber from the mass by gently pulling it free. You want a segment about 4–6 inches (10–15 cm) long and ½ inch (1.25 cm) wide.

What makes yarn

Fiber is turned into yarn by twist. Completely untwisted fiber will pull apart easily. Twisted fiber, or yarn, is strong and won't pull apart. The twist comes from the spindle, and the transformation takes place between your hands. What your hands do as this occurs is called drafting—letting the fibers slide past each other and then letting the twist catch them.

The size of your yarn is determined by how much fiber is caught by the twist. When spinning, your goal is to pay attention to the fiber which is

between your hands—the fiber that's about to become yarn. Everything else can take care of itself!

The first twist

Tie your starter yarn around the long portion of the spindle's shaft, next to the whorl. Turn the spindle a few times in the direction of the arrow, so the yarn wraps around the shaft. Take the starter yarn through the hook or notch at the top of the spindle (on a bottom-whorl spindle that doesn't have a hook or groove, make a half-hitch about ½ inch [1.25 cm] below the tip of the shaft).

A top-whorl spindle can hang from the starter yarn. Ultimately a bottom-whorl spindle will do the same, but while you're learning, rest it on a table so it doesn't fall.

Your lower hand will rotate the spindle and release the twist. Your upper hand will hold the unspun fiber, gently prepare it to become yarn, and then keep the twist from moving into the fiber before you want it to.

Spin the spindle in the direction of

the arrow; hold the loose end of the starter yarn with your upper hand and watch the twist collect in the yarn.

Feather out one end of your fiber and overlap it onto the starter yarn. Pinch the fiber and yarn together with your lower hand, and pinch just above that point with your upper hand.

Rotate the spindle with your lower hand, then move that hand back up to its "pinch" position. Don't worry much about what the spindle's doing; the only thing you don't want it to do right now is to turn backwards, away from the arrow, and "untwist" your work. It's okay if the spindle flops over to one side after it has rotated, or even if you stop it. As long as there's twist in the starter yarn for you to work with, that's fine.

Move your upper hand a little way up the fiber, pulling gen-

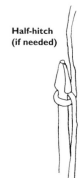

Half-hitch (if needed)

tly to loosen the fiber between your hands. Then pinch the fiber with your upper hand and slide the lower hand up next to it. The twist will glide up behind your lower hand. You've just made yarn!

Continuing to spin

That's it. Your hands repeat the *pinch, pull, slide* movements, while your lower hand occasionally reaches down to rotate the spindle. As you practice, you'll feel at first like too much is going on at once. Then you'll find that your yarn is strong and your hands know what they're doing, so you don't have to stop the spindle while you draft.

Soon after that you'll think that you're reaching a long way down to rotate the spindle, and you'll find yourself with between 2 and 3 feet (50 and 75 cm) of yarn that you have made. It's time to wind on.

Winding on

To keep your yarn from tangling while you wind on, catch it behind your elbow. Release the end from the hook or half-hitch and turn the spindle (always in the same direction) so the new yarn wraps around the spindle shaft, over the initial wraps of the starter yarn. Leave enough new yarn free to catch in the hook or to make a new half-hitch. That's it—back to spinning!

When you run out of fiber in your hand, take a new piece and feather out one of its ends. Feather out the end of the old piece as well, overlap the two ends, and let them twist together in a join.

Bumps and breaks

Lumps happen in yarn when there's too much fiber between your fingers at the time that the twist comes along and turns it into yarn. Make sure your lower hand is pinching back the twist until your upper hand has pulled out the fiber and gotten it ready.

Breaks occur when there's too little fiber in that spot between your fingers.

Fix a break by feathering the end of the yarn and the end of your fiber and making a new join.

Thick-and-thin can be a design element in fancy yarns. While you're learning, experiment a bit with these extremes so you can see how they occur and can later produce them when you want to.

Winding off

After a while, you'll have a cop of yarn that fills the spindle—the spindle feels heavier to work with, and the yarn begins to get in your way when you rotate the shaft. It's time to wind your yarn off into a skein. Here's a handy way to do that:

Tie the skein with small pieces of yarn (the two ends of your spinning will do; a third tie is helpful).

Set the twist by running some lukewarm water in a sink, setting your skein on the water, and gently pressing the skein so it is submerged. Leave it for a few minutes, lift it out, squeeze

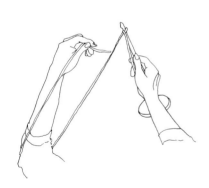

When your yarn gets long, you need to wind on. To keep the strand from tangling while you do this, catch it behind your elbow. release the end nearest the spindle and wind the yarn around the spindle shaft.

Join

To join new fiber, feather out the ends of the new and old fiber supplies, overlap them, and let them twist together.

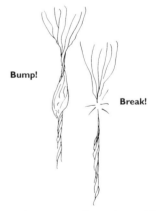

Bump! **Break!**

Blumps or lumps occur when a clump of fiber gets caught by the twist. Breaks happen when there's too little fiber to maintain the yarn's integrity.

gently to remove some of the water, and hang it over a faucet or doorknob to drip dry.

Congratulations! You're a spinner. There are many more things to learn about spinning—like how to make plied yarns and designer yarns, how to spin all sorts of different fibers, and what to do with your yarn (if you want to do more than pat and admire it)—but you've just crossed the threshold.

Making yarn

Many kinds of spinning tools are available today—everything from simple wooden hand spindles to high-tech electric spinners, from antique wool and flax wheels to modern wheels. The diversity of spinning tools is a wonderful story in itself, but it's important to remember that in **handspinning**, it's the skill and sensitivity of the spinner's hands that shapes the yarn. The spinner is in control; the tool is just an assistant.

No matter which tool you use, the

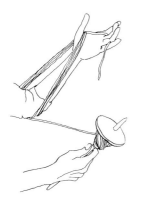

When your spindle's full, you can wind a skein around your forearm. Start with the movement on page 87, and continue as shown above.

process of spinning is basically the same. The first step is **drafting** or pulling fibers out of the prepared lock, top, batt, or roving. Drafting just a few fibers at a time makes a very thin yarn; drafting many fibers makes a thicker yarn. **Twisting** the drafted fibers makes yarn. Twist holds the fibers together so they don't slip apart or rub loose; one of the spinner's skills is determining the appropriate amount of twist for a given yarn. At the start, you want enough twist that the yarn is strong . . . and not so much that the strand you are spinning makes itself into independent corkscrews. After drafting and twisting a length of yarn, you can let it **wind onto** the bobbin of the spinning wheel or wind it onto a spindle by hand, then start drafting and twisting more yarn. When you finish spinning one batch of fiber, you make a **join** by splicing on a new supply. A careful join is invisible in the finished yarn.

Turn the wheel (or spindle) one way and you get **Z-twist** yarn. Turn it the other way and you'll have **S-twist** yarn. By convention, most spinners turn the wheel clockwise (Z) to make yarn from loose fiber, but the only rule is that if you *start* spinning in a given direction you need to keep going that way until you've finished with that bobbin- or spindle-full of yarn (reversing directions untwists your work).

Depending on what type of fiber you're spinning and how you use your hands, the steps of drafting and twisting may be done separately and in sequence, or they can flow together into a continuous process. Spinners working with combed, long-staple wool often draft by moving their hands just a few inches—about half the length of the fibers—in a gesture called a **short draw**. Then they deliberately guide the twist into the drafted fibers, making a

smooth, dense **worsted** yarn. Spinners using short-staple wool that has been carded and rolled into rolags may use a **long draw**, moving one hand back and forth with a full swing of the arm, simultaneously drafting and twisting up to three feet of fuzzy, puffy, **woolen** yarn before winding it on. You'll see many variations and combinations of these techniques if you watch different people spin; as with most decisions in spinning, what's "right" is whatever works best for the individual spinner and the fiber. Because they can be so unique, there is no precise, consistent way of describing drafting methods.

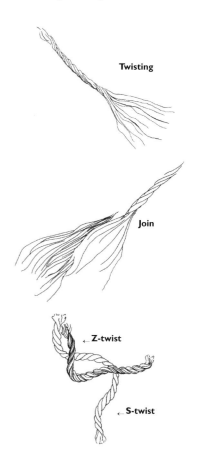

Twisting

Join

← **Z-twist**

← **S-twist**

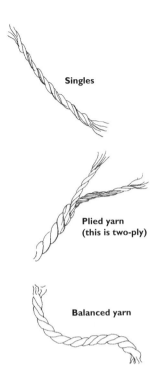

Singles

Plied yarn
(this is two-ply)

Balanced yarn

When you turn loose fiber into yarn, you make a **singles** yarn (a single strand), with the fibers all twisted in the same direction. Singles yarn can be finished and used as is, but spinners often take an extra step, twisting two or more strands of singles together to make **plied** yarn, which is usually stronger, more uniform, and easier to handle. The simplest plied yarn twists two singles together in the opposite direction to their original spinning (Z singles, S plied). A **balanced** yarn is a special type of plied yarn, where the twist used in plying exactly balances the twist used in spinning and straightens out the fibers. A balanced yarn is very calm and doesn't kink at all.

Basic spinning and plying techniques produce "plain vanilla" yarn,

lovely in itself and useful for all kinds of knitting, weaving, and other projects. A plain-vanilla spinner can achieve plenty of variety simply by using different types of wool (in natural or dyed colors), by varying the thickness and twist of the singles, and by choosing whether or not to ply the yarn. For even more variety, there are advanced techniques for making fancy **designer** yarns, with unique texture and color effects.

Finishing wool yarn

After plying—or after spinning, if the yarn will be used as singles—make the yarn into a skein by winding it onto a **niddy-noddy** or **skein winder**. Tie the skein in at least three places before you remove it from the niddy-noddy. Wool yarn usually gets softer and puffier when you wash and dry it, and it also **shrinks** in length—usually 10 to 25 percent, but sometimes even more. It's a good idea to wash yarn and let it shrink before you knit, weave, or do something else with it.

To **wash** the skein, fill your sink with comfortably warm water and add a squirt or two of dishwashing liquid or shampoo; set the skein on top of the

water and press it down gently to get it wet. Let it soak for a few minutes. Lift the skein out of the water, drain the basin, and run in rinse water of the same temperature. Set the skein in the water and press down gently again. Remove the skein, drain the water, and repeat the rinse. Squeeze the skein (don't wring it) to remove excess water, and then let the skein dry on a towel or rack.[3]

Felting happens when you agitate or rub wet wool fleece, yarn, or fabric. It's wonderful to make felt on purpose, but to avoid accidental felting when you're washing any wool product, be careful to handle it as little and as gently as possible.

If the yarn looks wrinkly or kinky after you wash it, you can smooth it out by **steaming** it, like you would steam wrinkles out of a garment. Use a travel steamer or steam iron, or pass the skein over the spout of a steaming teakettle; five to ten seconds of steaming is enough to smooth most yarns.

Admire your skein. It's some of the best yarn in the world!

[3] The same process works for washing raw wool. Wash in batches that fit your sink or basin, and gently lift the wool mass as you would a skein.

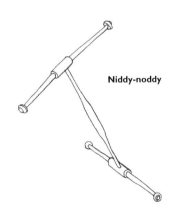

Niddy-noddy

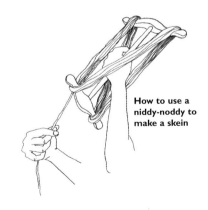

How to use a niddy-noddy to make a skein

ACKNOWLEDGMENTS

Contributors

These people generously contributed intelligence, enthusiasm, knowledge, and effort to make the Save the Sheep project possible. If we've missed anyone, let us know!

Dobree Adams, Kentucky
Heather Adamson, Manitoba, Canada
Nancy Alegria, California
Algonquin Spinners, Ohio
Carol Amidon, Ohio
Diana Andrew, United Kingdom
Mary Ann Anton, Maine
Jeannine Bakriges, Vermont
Vicki Ball, Vermont
Barbara Ballas, Oregon
Diane Ballerino-Regan, North Carolina
Elizabeth Barnes, Pennsylvania
Nancy Barnett, Missouri
Lena Benally, Arizona
Diane Bentley-Baker, Texas
Joan Berner, New York
Betty Beshoar, Kentucky
Johanna Bolton, Florida
Laurie Boltz, Wisconsin
Margaret Boos, California
Andrea Bottone, New York
Sandy Bousman, Wyoming
Laurie Boyer, Illinois
Barbara Bradley, Idaho
Diane Braun, Arizona
Beverly Brookhart, North Carolina
Joan Brown, Manitoba, Canada
Brenda Bryon, United Kingdom
Maureen Burnett, Mississippi
Jane Burton, Missouri
Deb Bury, New Hampshire
Beth Caddell, Indiana
Joy Cain, Ohio
Holly Carter, Ohio
Randy Chelsey, California

Jo Coad, Ohio
Rhonda Colcord-Durant, New Hampshire
Kaye Collins, Colorado
Joan Contraman, Montana
Anne Cook, Scotland
Karen Cook, New Hampshire
Donna Jo Copeland, Indiana
Mary Ellen ("Melon") Corsini, North Carolina
Jackie Cravens, Tennessee
Christine Crossman, New York
Linda Cummings, Pennsylvania
Laura Cunningham, California
Pia Cusick, Alabama
Brigitte de March, Manitoba, Canada
Veronica de Olive-Lowe, New Zealand
Eileen Ditsler, California
Victoria Downing, Oregon
Martha Driscoll, Massachusetts
Cindy Earls, Tennessee
Baerbel Epprecht, Germany
Jackie Erickson-Schweitzer, Louisiana
Deb Essen, Montana
Florence Feldman-Wood, Massachusetts
Ingrid Fingal, Arizona
Cherry Fitzgibbon, British Columbia, Canada
Trygve Fjarli, Norway
Karen Ford, Alabama
Stephanie Fore, Missouri
Cathy Forgit, Minnesota
Gail Former, Indiana
Robin Fouquette, California
Jeanie Fraas, Nebraska
Friendship Spinners, Kentucky

Teresa Gardner, Missouri
Elke Gehrke, Germany
Mary Geier, Alabama
Linda Geiger, New York
Cheryl Geist-Brozell, Pennsylvania
Priscilla Gibson-Roberts, Colorado
Alice Gillespie, Pennsylvania
Polly Givens, Ohio
Kimberly Godsey, Oregon
Sue Goudy, New Mexico
Suzi Gough, APO/United Kingdom
Barbara Gower, Alabama
Greater Birmingham Fiber Guild, Alabama
Michelle Green, England
Sandy Gunzberg, Maryland
Rosemary Harrison, Pennsylvania
Rita Padilla Haufmann, New Mexico
Kate Hedstrom, New Jersey
Cynthia Heeren, Oregon
Margaret Hermann, New Mexico
Cathy Hopkins, Pennsylvania
Layl Horton, Arizona
Martin Hughes, Ontario, Canada
Pat Huskey, California
Indiana Shetland Sheep Breeders Association, Indiana
Frances Irving, Manitoba, Canada
Suzy Ivan, Michigan
Judy Ede Jackson, Utah
Carol James, Manitoba, Canada
Joan Jenness, Maine
Cathy Johnson, New Mexico
Gail Johnson, Minnesota
Liz Johnson, Utah

Nancy Johnston, Arizona
Suzanne Jones, Missouri
Mary Kaiser, Alabama
Phyllis Karsten, California
Mary Kay, Scotland
Betty Kelly, New Zealand
Jacquie Kelly, Arizona
Jane Kennedy, Oregon
Karen Kuckenbecker, Wisconsin
Sara Lamb, California
Ann Lambert, Ontario, Canada
Catherine Lampman, Tennessee
Maralyn Larson, Idaho
Joan LeClair, Wisconsin
Debra M. Lee, Tennessee
Judi Lehrhaupt, Pennsylvania
Carole Lentz, Michigan
Dave Lewis, Ohio
Marla Lewis, Indiana
Debra Leyh, New Jersey
Ann Lien, South Dakota
Joanne Littler, Vermont
Robin Lynde, California
Mariah Mabee, Missouri
Manitoba Handspinners, Manitoba,
    Canada
Terry Martin, Alabama
Debra Mase, Tennessee
Heather Maxey, British Columbia,
    Canada
May Frances McCay, New Jersey
Deborah McClintock, Delaware
Joan McFadyen, Wisconsin
Eugenie McGuire, California
Katie McLaughlin, Virginia
Marie Mercuri, Illinois
Susan Anne Metz, Missouri
Robin Metzger, Oregon
Middle Tennessee Fiber Guild,
    Tennessee
Andrea Mielke, Wisconsin
Marjorie Mills, Michigan
Winifred Moore, California
Anne-Marie Moroney, Ireland
Nanette Mosher, Illinois
Noreen Muellerweiss, Michigan

Jean Newsted, Alberta, Canada
Amanda Nikkel, Kentucky
Pat Noah, Colorado
Sammie Oaks, New Mexico
Rindy (Lorinda) O'Brien, Maine
Mary Oehlstrom, Ohio
Kathrin Olson-Rutz, Montana
Barbara Osborne, California
Kris Paige, Wisconsin
Llyn Payne, Oregon
Elsbeth Pears, United Kingdom
Esther K. Peregrine, Illinois
Kris Peters, Pennsylvania
Janet Petty, Arizona
Judy Phillips, Oregon
Rita Piatt, Missouri
Patricia Piehota, Oklahoma
Sara Gene Posnett, Pennsylvania
Danette Pratt, Ohio
Barbara Puett, Wyoming
Deborah Pulliam, Maine
Karen Noll Purucker, New Mexico
Colleen Reid, California
Catherine Reimers, New York
Beka Rewerts, Germany
Carol Rhoades, Texas
Susan Richards, Maine
Rae Jean Rimmer, Virginia
Renée Robertson, Michigan
Dorothy Robinson, Alberta, Canada
Gayle Roehm, Maryland
Ruth Wade Ruggiero, Pennsylvania
Francine Ruiter, Manitoba, Canada
Norma Sanders, England
Niki Sawyer, New York
Joan Schneiber, New Jersey
Sharon Schulz, North Dakota
Cathy Scott, Indiana
Debbie Scott, Alabama
Joanne Seiff, North Carolina
Ann Sheffield, Pennsylvania
Shetland Guild of Spinners, Dyers,
    Weavers, Scotland
Peggy Siders, Indiana
Anne Silk, Prince Edward Island,
    Canada

Margaret Sjostrom, Alberta, Canada
Edna Smith, Alberta, Canada
Mary Spahr, Ohio
Mary Spanos, Alabama
Spindle and Dyepot Guild, Wisconsin
D. Phillip Sponenberg, Virginia
Barbara Kent Stafford, California
Patricia Stein, Germany
Kris Sudduth, Texas
Ellen Sullivan, California
Tan Summers, Utah
Sarah Swett, Idaho
Elizabeth Syron, Louisiana
Sara Syron, Louisiana
Jo-Anne Tabachek, Manitoba, Canada
Connie Taylor, New Mexico
Gwena Tessier, California
Eva Thatcher, North Carolina
Suzanne Tietjen, Illinois
Laura Todd, Oregon
Ann Tomes, Massachusetts
Tri-Community Adult Education
    Weaving and Spinning Class,
    Covina, California
Mary Underwood, Michigan
Sandra Van Liew, Oregon
Nancy Van Tassel, California
Jacqueline Vaughan, Michigan
Marie Villareal, California
Jan Viren, Minnesota
Ruth Volden, Norway
Mieke von Massow, Manitoba, Canada
Emily Walker, Texas
Victoria Warden, Ohio
Kathy Watts, California
Diane Waugh, New Jersey
Susan Weaver, Pennsylvania
Alexandra Weikert, Germany
Anne Williams, Connecticut
Martha E. Williams, Iowa
Rita Williams, Missouri
Susan Winkler, Kentucky
Edna Wooler, Manitoba, Canada
Vicki Yost, Colorado
Aurelia Young, Michigan

Sponsors

These people sponsored the jurying of the Save the Sheep traveling exhibit, providing space, food, and support for the challenging process of developing a selection of pieces which represented the rich array of possibilities.

Solveig Lark, **Gallery East**, 229 E. 10th St., Loveland, CO 80538

Shirley Ellsworth, **Lambspun of Colorado**, 1101 E. Lincoln Ave., Fort Collins, CO 80524

Jane Fournier, **New Zealand Timber Spindles**, 2021 Winne Ave., Helena, MT 59601

Karen Kinyon, **Double K Diamond Llamas**, 2933 E. Mulberry St., Fort Collins, CO 80524

Special thanks to Vicky Heitman and to **McKee Conference & Wellness Center**, 2000 N. Boise Ave., Loveland, CO 80538. They found us a generous amount of space for jurying at the last minute when it became obvious that the number of entries exceeded the capacity of the Interweave Press conference room by a factor of about six.

Resources

For further informatiuon on the history of spinning or rare breeds of sheep, here are some sources. The history publications were collected by Susan Strawn Bailey and contributed to her essay, "A Glimpse into the History of Handspinning."

Rare breeds and domesticated animals in general

Alderson, Lawrence. *The Chance to Survive.* Northamptonshire, U.K.: Pilkington Press, 1994.

Bixby, Donald E., Carolyn J. Christman, Cynthia J. Ehrman, and D. Phillip Sponenberg. *Taking Stock: The North American Livestock Census.* Blacksburg, Virginia: The McDonald & Woodward Publishing Company, 1994.

Budiansky, Stephen. *The Covenant of the Wild: Why Animals Chose Domestication.* Leesburg, Virginia: The Terrapin Press, 1995. Previously published by William Morrow, 1992.

Caras, Roger A. *A Perfect Harmony: The Intertwining Lives of Animals and Humans throughout History.* New York: Simon and Schuster, 1996.

Christman, Carolyn J., D. Phillip Sponenberg, and Donald E. Bixby. *A Rare Breeds Album of American Livestock.* Pittsboro, North Carolina: The American Livestock Breeds Conservancy, 1997.

Clutton-Brock, Juliet. *A Natural History of Domesticated Mammals.* Austin: University of Texas Press, 1987.

Dowling, Robert, Lawrence Alderson, and Roger A. Caras. *Rare Breeds.* Boston and New York: Little, Brown, 1994.

Fournier, Jane, and Nola Fournier. *In Sheep's Clothing: A Handspinner's Guide to Wools.* Loveland, Colorado: Interweave Press, 1995.

Gnatkowski, Janice. *167 International Sheep Breeds.* Carrizozo, New Mexico: Janice Gnatkowski, (1978).

Hart, Edward. "Galway Sheep: The latest breed to come under our wing." *The Ark* 24, no. 2 (Summer 1996): 70.

Hunt, Jeremy. "The Teeswater." *The Ark* 26, no. 3 (Autumn 1998): 114–15.

Latham, Harry. "The British Wool Marketing Board: A miracle of organization." *The Ark* 26, no. 3 (Autumn 1998): 109–111.

Lutwyche, Richard. "From Sheep to Shawl: A look at the Natural Fibre Company." *The Ark* 26, no. 2 (Summer 1998): 60–61.

Oklahoma State University livestock resource web site, www.ansi.okstate.edu/BREEDS/SHEEP/.

Raloff, Janet. "Dying Breeds: Livestock are developing a largely unrecognized biodiversity crisis." *Science News: The Weekly Newsmagazine of Science* 152, no. 14 (Oct. 4, 1997): 211, 216–18.

Ryder, Michael L. "The Hebridean Blackface or Boreray Sheep of St. Kilda." *The Ark* 24, no. 2 (Summer 1996): 62–63.

Skinner, J. B., D. E. Lord, and J. M. Williams, eds. *British Sheep and Wool.* West Yorkshire, U.K.: The British Wool Marketing Board, 1985.

Webb, Penny, and Cathy Seagrave. "Discovering North Ronaldsays." *The Ark* 26, no. 2 (Summer 1998).

Selected rare-breed articles in Spin-Off

Includes only general articles on breeds and associated cultural traditions. See Spin-Off indexes, by breed, for articles showing projects made of a specific wool. The indexes are available from Interweave Press (contact information on page 96) or online at www.interweave.com.

Alderman, Sharon D. "The Return of the Churro." Vol. 8, no. 1 (Spring 1984): 46–48.

Altergott, Sharon. "Shetlands invade America!" Vol. 11, no. 2 (Summer 1987): 54. *Records what was likely the first importation of true Shetlands to North America. Look how far they've come!*

Bailey, Susan Strawn. "Two Grey Hills Weaving Museum: In the middle of everywhere." Vol. 23, no. 2 (Summer 1999): 24–25. *Short article on regional style of Navajo weaving dependent on natural-colored Navajo Churro fleece.*

Cathey, Sue. "Fiber Basics: Tunis Sheep." Vol. 22, no. 4 (Winter 1998): 44–47.

Champion, Ellen. "Karakul: A Tale of Three Rugs (two of them handspun)." Vol. 13, no. 4 (Winter 1989): 27–28.

Clarke, Amy C. "K'un K'un: The story of a cooperative." Vol. 23, no. 1 (Spring 1999): 76–79.

_____. "Save the Sheep Project Results." Vol. 24, no. 1 (Spring 2000): 40–43.

Daurelle, Jude. "The Spinning Nuns of Shaw Island." Vol. 22, no. 4 (Winter 1998): 73–76. *They keep Cotswolds.*

Farlam, Gill. "The Manx Loghtan." Vol. 14, no. 1 (Spring 1990): 56–57.

Fournier, Jane. "Fiber Basics: English Leicester." Vol. 16, no. 2 (Summer 1992): 25–27.

_____. "Fiber Basics: Icelandic Wool." Vol. 23, no. 1 (Spring 1999): 64–68. *Icelandic sheep are double-coated, come in a number of colors and not endangered. Principles for using this fleece apply to working with the wool of a number of the endangered breeds.*

_____. "Fiber Basics: Wensleydale." Vol. 19, no. 3 (Fall 1995): 46–48.

_____. "How to Handle a Whole Fleece." Vol. 23, no. 1 (Spring 1999): 48–52. *Working with raw wool.*

_____. "Fiber Basics: Shetland." Vol. 16, no. 4 (Winter 1992): 25–29.

Fournier, Nola. "Fiber Basics: Dorset Down." Vol. 23, no. 2 (Summer 1999): 38–43.

George, Mother Hildegard, OSB. "Rare Breeds in a Benedictine Monastery." Vol. 22, no. 4 (Winter 1998): 77–78.

Leadbeater, Eliza. "Native British Sheep: The Rare Breeds." Vol. 3 (annual, 1979): 28–31.

Lightfoot, Amy. "Primitive Norwegian Sheep." Vol. 13, no. 3 (Fall 1989): 55–57.

McNeal, Nancy Wilkie. "Navajo Sheep Project: A Survivor!" Vol. 17, no. 2 (Summer 1993): 35, 37.

Moroney, Anne-Marie. "Galway Sheep." Vol. 14, no. 3 (Fall 1990): 36–37.

Muller, Donna. "The Sacred Sheep of Chiapas." Vol. 23, no. 1 (Spring 1999): 80–85. *See also Amy Clarke's "K'un K'un Cooperative." Chiapas sheep do not have a registry and are therefore not identified as a breed. In many other regards, their situation parallels that of the endangered breeds.*

_____. "Sarah Natani: A Year with Navajo Sheep." Vol. 16, no. 4 (Winter 1992): 40–45. *An example of the balances between people, place, and a specific breed of sheep.*

Murray, Gwen B. "Breeds of Sheep for Spinners: Cotswold." Vol. 11, no. 1 (Spring 1987): 47.

"Navajo Sheep Project." Vol. 10, no. 2 (Summer 1986): 6.

"Navajo Sheep Project Update." Vol. 8, no. 2 (Summer 1984): 6.

Neill, Norma. "Spinning in the Western Isles." Vol. 19, no. 2 (Summer 1995): 68–70.

Olberding, Susan Deaver. "Churro Sheep: A Southwest Legacy." Vol. 17, no. 2 (Summer 1993): 34, 36–37.

Painter, Ingrid. "Spotting a Good Jacob." Vol. 7. no. 2 (Summer 1983): 18–21.

Pulliam, Deborah. "Fiber Basics: Cotswold." Vol. 23, no. 4 (Winter 1999): 44–50.

Robson, Deborah. "Diné bé 'Iiná': The Navajo Lifeway." Vol. 20, no. 4 (Winter 1996): 82–85.

_____. "Rare Wools from Rare Sheep, Part 1: Why endangered sheep matter to spinners." Vol. 23, no. 1 (Spring 1999): 90–94. *The first of two articles giving comprehensive background for the Save the Sheep project. Summarizes breeds listed as rare, endangered, and minority by The American Livestock Breeds Conservancy and the Rare Breeds Survival Trust, with as much information on fleece quality as was available at the time.*

_____. "Rare Wools from Rare Sheep, Part 2: Why endangered sheep matter to spinners." Vol. 23, no. 1 (Spring 1999): 90–94. *The second of two articles giving comprehensive background for the Save the Sheep project. This article appears in this book in a different format (pages 6–13).*

Sayres, Meghan Nuttall. "Tierra Wools." Vol. 23, no. 2 (Summer 1999):

84–88. *Navajo Churro wool and traditional weaving techniques form the basis of this New Mexico cooperative.*

Scott, Barbara Carter. "The Shetlands' Fine Tradition." Vol. 13, no. 4 (Winter 1989): 58–66. *Shetland sheep, spinning, and shawls.*

Szostak, Rosemarie. "Soay: Stone-Age Fiber." Vol. 19, no. 2 (Summer 1995): 62–65.

Walker, Linda Berry. "Know Your Sheep Breeds: Jacob." Vol. 14, no. 1 (Spring 1990): 20, 22.

_____. "Know Your Sheep Breeds: Karakul." Vol. 13, no. 4 (Winter 1989): 27.

_____. "Know Your Sheep Breeds: Lincoln." Vol. 12, no. 4 (Winter 1988): 8–9.

_____. "To Save a Sheep, Spin Its Fleece." Vol. 14, no. 1 (Spring 1990): 21.

Williams, Kathy. "Progress and Priorities: Always a Question of Balance." Vol. 20, no. 4 (Winter 1996): 86–87. *The challenges of marketing and sustainable economics for people who keep Navajo Churro sheep on the Navajo Nation.*

History of handspinning

American Wool Council. "The History of Wool." Englewood, Colorado: American Sheep Industry Association, 1993.

Anderson, Enid. *The Spinner's Encyclopedia.* Devon, U.K.: David & Charles, 1987.

Baines, Patricia. *Linen Hand Spinning and Weaving.* London: B. T. Batsford, 1989.

Burnham, Dorothy K. *The Comfortable Arts: Traditional Spinning and Weaving in Canada.* Ottawa: The National Museums of Canada, 1981.

Carminati, Cheryl C. "The Shakers and Spinning." *Spin-Off* 13, no. 4 (Winter 1989): 30–31.

Crockett, Candace. *The Complete Spinning Book.* New York: Watson-Guptill, 1977.

Fannin, Allen. *Handspinning: Art and Technique.* New York: Litton Educational Publishing, 1970.

Gauldie, Enid. *Spinning and Weaving.* Edinburgh: National Museums of Scotland, 1995.

Gibson-Roberts, Priscilla. *High Whorling.* Cedaredge, Colorado: Nomad Press, 1998.

Hecht, Ann. *The Art of the Loom.* New York: Rizzoli International Publications, 1989.

Langley, Susan B. M. "The Origins of Sericulture in Early China." *Spin-Off* 18, no. 2 (Summer 1994): 100–02.

Marks, Paula Mitchell. *Hands to the Spindle.* College Station, Texas: Texas A & M University Press, 1996.

Ross, Mabel. *The Encyclopedia of Hand Spinning.* London: B. T. Batsford, 1988.

Organizations

United States. **The American Livestock Breeds Conservancy,** PO Box 477, Pittsboro, NC 27312, (919) 542-5704, fax (919) 545-0022; www.albc-usa.org/, albc@albc-usa.org. *Founded in 1977 (as the American Minor Breeds Conservancy) to conserve rare breeds and genetic diversity in livestock.*

Canada. **Rare Breeds Canada,** c/o Trent University Environmental and Resource Studies Program, Peterborough, ON, Canada K9J 7B8, phone (705) 748-1634, rarebreedscanada@trentu.ca,

www.flora.org/rbc/. *A federally incorporated charitable organization. Website is not large but is charming, well designed, and provides useful links to other organizations.*

United Kingdom. **Rare Breeds Survival Trust,** Freepost, National Agricultural Centre, Stoneleigh Park, Warwickshire CV8 2BR, phone 01203 696551, fax 01203 696706.

Australia. **The Australian Rare and Minority Breeds Association,** Inc., 264 Old Spring Valley Road, Flowerdale,

Victoria 3717, Australia, phone/fax 61 3 5473 3491, mullens@castlemaine.net.au, people.enternet.com.au/~cherylh/index.htm. *Nonprofit organization founded in 1992.*

New Zealand. **Rare Breeds Conservation Society of New Zealand,** Inc., P. Kuehn Waitangi, RD 2 Kaituna, Christchurch, New Zealand.

Europe/International. **Pro Specie Rara,** Engelgasse 12a, CH-9000 St. Gallen, Switzerland.

INDEX OF NAMES

Get Spinning
with ⊞ INTERWEAVE PRESS

SPIN·OFF magazine is pure spinning satisfaction. Show and tell with the world's most creative spinners will inspire you. Solid, accurate technical information, plus tips and tricks for a lifetime of spinning will add new facets to your spinning know how. Our coverage and celebration of the spinning community will connect you with other spinners who share your passion. Spin with SPIN·OFF, your hands will say ahhh and your brain will say ah-hah! How can you spin without it? Published quarterly 800-767-9638.

A Handspindle Treasury
20 Years of Spinning Wisdom from SPIN·OFF *Magazine*

SPIN·OFF has compiled 20 years of the best and most useful knowledge on handspindles from past issues. Everything you need to know on handspindle use, techniques, and tricks.

8½ × 11, paperbound, 88 pages, color photos and line drawings. #1038—$16.95

Color in Spinning
Deb Menz

For the handspinner seeking new adventures in color, the extensive photos of dyed spun fiber and the step-by-step processes make this book an inspiration as well as a reference.

8½ × 11, hardbound, 240 pages, over 300 color and b&w illustrations. #690—$39.95

800-272-2193
www.interweave.com